THIS PSYCHIC PROPHETIC AGE

by

Pam Vinnett

Vincom, Inc.
Tulsa, Oklahoma

This Psychic Prophetic Age
ISBN 0-927936-65-8

P. O. Box 702400
Tulsa, OK 74170

Published by Vincom, Inc.
P. O. Box 702400
Tulsa, OK 74170
(918) 254-1276

Printed in the United States of America.

Dedication

I lovingly dedicate this book to the memory of my mother, Mrs. Dorothy Wigfall Green, a prophetess of the Lord, who departed this life in April, 1994. At her memorial service, her dedicated pastor, friend and bishop, Dr. Norman Wagner, eulogized her with the message, "A Greater Than Miriam Was Here."

Acknowledgements

I gratefully acknowledge my wonderful grandfather and grandmother, the late Rufus and Hattie Wigfall; my wonderful father, Attorney William Green; siblings and spouses, Michael and Karen Green, Jeffrey and Cheryl Green; and "Mamma" Flossie Vinnett, for their love, prayers and encouragement.

I acknowledge my PITS (prophets in training): Brenda Todd, Roberta Jones, Ava Fox, Donald Ausby, Doyle Tucker and Janine Burns.

With special gratitude, I acknowledge: Pastor Phillip and Sylvia Imler; Bishop Bill and Shirley McKinney; Pastor Carlton and Gina Pearson; Pastor Clarence and Margaret Vinnett; Dr. E. Bernard and Debra Jordan; Dr. Paula Price; Prophetess Jeanne Wilkerson who has gone on to glory; Pastors Billy Joe and Sharon Daugherty; Dr. Myles Munroe; and Pastors Jefferson and Debra Edwards.

Acknowledgements

Contents

Contents

Foreword by Carlton Pearson

I first became familiar with Pam Vinnett when her husband George, then single, was my road manager and public relations director in the early 80s.

Pam became a subject of conversation after George and I encountered her mother, the late Dorothy Green, on the closing night of a week-long revival in the 19th Street Baptist Church in Washington, DC, pastored by Dr. Jerry Moore.

George was standing beside me as a long line of inquirers rushed toward us for final prayers and altar ministry on the last evening of the services we had been conducting. Before either of us knew anything, Mrs. Green had pressed her way through the crowd, thrust her hand on my forehead and began prophesying before anyone could restrain her. Her words were loud, forceful and most distinct. At that time, I didn't know her, but I could immediately recognize she was of God. Her words rang, reverberated and echoed deep down within my soul.

I don't remember what she said verbatim, but I could never forget the "spirit of prophecy" under which she spoke. That spirit has had a lasting effect on both my life and ministry ever since.

Some years later, Pam and George married and are now a blessing as elders in our body. Pam continues the rich tradition established by her mother, functioning as a prophetess, and has edified our church and the body in general, repeatedly.

Pam met and prophesied to my wife Gina two months before I met and fell in love with her. In fact, she introduced us and the rest for us has been divine and ordained history.

God spoke to my heart in January, 1990, and instructed me to release the spirit of prophecy in our church. Since then, both the spiritual posture and complexion of our church has changed dramatically. Jesus the Prophet lives and moves freely in our house and has thus put all other spirits under divine indictment, particularly the spirit of fear.

Of the five-fold ministry gifts recorded in Ephesians 4:11, prophecy seems to be, for most people, the more intimidating. I suppose it is because it is the more mystical or one might even call it the most mysterious of the group. The pastor, teacher and evangelist throughout this century have been continually accepted and active, and the apostle is erroneously considered by many to be extinct. However, prophets and prophecy have always been eyed with suspicion, distrust, or at best, with apprehension or fear.

Because of this continual disdain for the gift of prophecy or the office and function of the prophet, the enemy has produced and found license to create his own counterfeit.

When Paul says in 1 Thessalonians 5:20 KJV, **Despise not prophesyings** (*The New International Version* says, **Do not treat prophecies with contempt**), or when he encourages us toward eagerness to prophesy in 1 Corinthians 14:39, he has particular reasons for his opinion, not the least of which is — If you restrain, restrict, or prohibit the "real thing" from its free and unadulterated expression — then the counterfeit, which is the devil's alternative, will rise up to take its place, seizing the opportunity afforded by the unmet need.

Isaiah 8:19 NIV says, **When men** [people] **tell you to consult mediums** [psychics] **and spiritists** [wizards], **who whisper and mutter, should not a people inquire of their God? Why consult the dead on behalf of the living?**

The *King James Version* translates the word *mediums* for "familiar spirits." It is the Hebrew word *Obe* from the Hebrew word *Ab* which is short for Abba "Daddy." It (Obe) expresses the idea of prattling a father's name, a mumble; i.e., a water skin from its hollow sound, hence a necromancer or a ventriloquist, as from a jar or bottle, etc. In other words, it's a voice from another source. Satan, as a ventriloquist, uses psychics as puppets through which he speaks. The psychics become, as it were, the water skin, bottle, or jar through which the hallow echo of a *SATANIC* utterance is spoken. It is a very dangerous and destructive thing and causes the person or people engaged in the practice to embrace a lying spirit and actually engage in the science and sin of spiritual intercourse with evil.

America, through this heinous and subtle practice, has opened its doors to an invasion of "familiar spirits" and confusing voices which have set this nation on a collision course with a spiritual holocaust.

I believe this book will help set the record straight by exposing the hidden agenda of the devil, but more importantly, by revealing the true plan of God in the gift and function of prophecy. The counterfeit will always appear genuine until the authentic is manifested.

As Paul says, **...when that which is perfect has come, then that which is in part will be done away** (1 Cor. 13:10).

I invite you for your own information and edification to research and read each scriptural reference in the Preface as well as the body of this book. It will increase your understanding of the content, and hopefully, enlarge your scope of God's view on the subject.

Preface

In writing a book on the prophetic, it is mandatory that there be an allowance of real life testimony, exposing bondages, and of course, liberty from them.

This testimony is a personal testimony of my family background. I believe that it will be an aid to bringing many people deliverance from demonic possession or oppression. Possibly as you read, you will see similarities in your background to mine and gain hope that your mother, father, sister, brother, or beloved one may also receive total liberty in Christ.

No person who is even remotely open to the supernatural became that way of their own accord. God, the Creator of all things, created every existing spirit (especially man) for His pleasure. Ancient demonic spirits have existed in the earth before the creation of man, and God was their Creator. (Gen. 3:1.) Although these wicked deities were not created evil, their choice to rebel against God caused evil to rise within them. (Ezek. 28:15.) All through the history of mankind, there is evidence of the intervention of demonic spirits, and of course, divine visitations from the Lord.

Man is an extraordinarily spiritual being. His true identity is that of a spirit occupying a clay house as we see in Genesis 1:26; 2:7. From the moment that God created man and woman, the chief enemy of mankind, Satan himself, sought to take possession of man and rule empires through him. Ezekiel 28:13-19 and Isaiah

14:12-20 speak of Satan, his plan and God's eventual plan for his final destruction. Revelation 20 says that a day will come when he will be cast into the pit of hell forever. But until that time, he will do all that is in his power to take as many men and women with him to ultimate destruction as possible.

God's desire, naturally, is to regain as many of His beloved children as possible to be with Him throughout eternity. Revelation 12:7-9 speaks of a war in heaven where a chief cherubim, Lucifer, was dispelled for rebelling against God. Approximately one-third of the angels joined the rebellion, and all were discharged into the cosmos, and then to earth. From that day until this, they have schemed to possess mankind with the distinct intention of breaking God's heart.

In Genesis 3:1-7 we see that man fell prey to his plan, but God, through a network of covenants and laws, designed a plan to regain man. Jesus Christ became the sacrifice to die for all men's sin that Satan could no longer prevail if they received that fact as truth and allowed Jesus to enter.

My grandparents, Rufus and Hattie Wigfall, were born in the rural South, in South Carolina. They were God-fearing people who received Jesus as Savior at an early age. However, for many blacks after the turn of the century into the late 20s, illiteracy was still at a high level. Grandpa improved his reading skills, as many others did, by reading a Bible.

The supernatural was a common part of society in that era. From as far back as Grandma could remember, it was confessed over her that she was a child that had "the eye" or the ability to see visions or have dreams that would come to pass. Every birth and death that happened to the people closest to my grandma in her lifetime, she dreamed beforehand. In fact, just before she died, she dreamed I had a son, and that she took his hand and went with him to a strange home with other children! At the time of her death, I had only one child, a girl. Within months of her death, I became pregnant with my second child, also a girl, and four months after delivering her, conceived my son. In between the last two births I moved into a new home. Grandma had seen it all. (At the time of her passing, I was preaching less than thirty miles from the town in which Grandma was born!)

My grandmother was actually a seer, or one who sees prophetically into some area of the supernatural. (1 Sam. 9:9.) Ignorance of the Word of God and no mentor to help develop the God-given call, she remained underdeveloped as far as her full potential. Neither she nor Grandpa ever aspired to the ministry, though their relationship with God and understanding of the Word was probably comparable to most of their pastors through the early years.

Grandpa had related to us many stories of the supernatural through our childhood years. We heard tales of witches who couldn't cross the doorsill of their family dwelling due to some prayer and preventive measures. And of course, the wonderful story of his conversion, praying for days alone in a secluded place, fasting, seeing a dove appear seemingly from nowhere, hearing God speak audibly, "You are My son."

No wonder satanic spirits were present in an obvious manner! There was from the roots of my family so much openness to the supernatural.

In later years of my grandparent's lives, after Mother was born, the background was set. Because Grandpa and Grandma were open to the supernatural,

Mother and her only sister were born open, so to speak. Demonic spirits, longing to access families, waited for years unable to successfully penetrate Grandma and Grandpa. Their salvation in their teen years, coupled with an open love for Jesus, protected them. However, Mother and her sister, though raised in the church, received an excellent education, and departed from what seemed to be the superstitions of the old way of religion. Though they embraced the church and were baptized at an early age, unclean spirits looked for any weak season to enter in.

And in they came, menacing my mother in troubled seasons of her life. She became an alcoholic, which, along with throat problems, destroyed a brilliant career as a classical singing artist. The ravages of sin took its toll upon her physical body which caused repeated hospital visits over the years. Daddy, a laid-back, hard-working attorney, simply created his own life, removing himself from three children and a wife with troubles. He buried himself in work and politics.

Once Mother, desperate for spiritual guidance, sought the council of a man who was a psychic medium. Her ignorance of spiritual forces in those days caused her to be unaware of the danger in that move.

My brothers and I, growing up, were besought by all kinds of spiritual forces, doors left open to us by parents and ancestors. Being introduced to board games at an early age got us in tune with the supernatural. No one knew that what was deemed as a harmless game was actually a chief door to an illegal entrance into the supernatural (only through God is there legal access)! This door allowed the oppressive forces of Satan to entice, then attack innocent children who were terribly open to spiritual things.

Soon my older brother and I entered a realm in the supernatural that caused us to astral project (when the spirit leaves the body, willingly or unwillingly), have dreams and be visited by spirits.

Allow me to say here that this is not an unusual occurrence for many children, particularly if there is a door opened. Some parents erroneously believe this kind of opening to the supernatural is God-inspired. This could not be further from the truth! The manifestations I described herein could only lead me and my siblings into witchcraft, or psychic administrations, had not Jesus Christ intervened. Psychic phenomena, root work (magical incantations combined with herbal remedies), divination (telling the future by magic), astrology and horoscopes (divining the future through the stars and planets [should this be called "horror-scopes"?]), palm reading, crystal ball gazing, gris-gris (spell casting), all are satanic according to the Word of God. (Deut. 18:10,11; 2 Kings 17:17; Jer. 14:4; Acts 16:16-18.)

> **There shall not be found among you anyone who makes his son or his daughter pass through the fire, or one who practices witchcraft, or a soothsayer, or one who interprets omens, or a sorcerer,**
>
> **Or one who conjures spells, or a medium, or a spiritist, or one who calls up the dead.**
>
> **Deuteronomy 18:10,11**

As adults, we children entered into drug abuse, alcoholism and lascivious living, choosing to shut God out except for funerals and weddings. Demonic visitations were so frequent that by my second year of college I had accepted them as a way of life. I began studying witchcraft in order to find a way of controlling the phenomenon. However, that study was short-lived when God began to awaken a Christian family friend at 3:00 a.m. every morning for months on end, to pray for me and my entire family's salvation! Suddenly, I turned from that course of study and began concentrating on my operatic career.

By my second year of graduate school, an amazing thing transpired. I had forfeited one-half year credit to change schools, moving closer to home when destiny prevailed — divine destiny. My oldest brother Michael had taken a business trip to a small Ohio town. Nowhere to go and nothing to do, he turned on the TV in his hotel room. Ben Kinchlow appeared on the scene, and after a few four-letter explicatives, was turned off. However, every channel he turned to played Ben Kinchlow of the 700 Club, speaking of Jesus and salvation! God had his attention by a supernatural occurrence, and moments later, the gentle giant of a man who is my brother, found himself knocked to the floor, prostrate, crying out to God for salvation and deliverance. God instantly changed and dramatically delivered him.

Just like the Apostle Paul, Mike returned preaching salvation. One by one, each of us received Jesus as personal Lord and Savior — and dramatic deliverance. Mother was saved by finding a Bible tract in a Methodist church. Father was saved being ministered to by Ben Kinchlow at a spiritual retreat. Brother Jeff was saved, being led to Christ by a minister who had just ministered to Dad, giving him an assurance of salvation. Jeff saw such a remarkable change in Dad, he asked to be saved. Karen, my sister-in-law, received Jesus at home at the same time Michael was being saved miles away!

The last to surrender was me. I had been home the week-end my mother was delivered from satanic spirits. Her deliverance was just as dramatic as that of the man in Mark 1:26 when Jesus delivered him of the unclean spirit. She shook the house, screamed a bloodcurdling cry and collapsed, only to rise seconds later with an indescribable glow, shouting, "I'm free." Within four months of her deliverance she was totally delivered from alcoholism (that day), legal chemical dependency, throat cancer, phlebitis, arthritis and much more!

Witnessing the dramatic changes in my family both frightened and thrilled me. Five months after my older brother's conversion, I surrendered my life to Jesus Christ. A full-blown alcoholic by then, I had moved to Cincinnati, Ohio, to work for the Cincinnati Opera Company. However, the vivid memory of mother's deliverance and change, coupled with that of my brother and his wife, as well as my father, haunted my waking hours.

I was in the middle of making an important decision concerning my career and future when a deep depression hit, followed by an alcoholic binge. Alone in my apartment on my 26th birthday, intoxicated, I called home to commiserate with my best friends, Mom and Dad. But to my amazement, she and Dad didn't commiserate with me. They told me, "All you need is Jesus." That night over the phone, I received Him as my Lord and Savior and was instantly delivered from alcoholism.

The next six months saw me delivered from every demonic oppression or possession, and for the first time since I could remember, there were no more evil, menacing supernatural experiences.

I entered an intense study of the Word, received the baptism of the Holy Spirit (Acts 2:1-4, as all my family had), and within one year's time, I'd accepted the call to the ministry. Every member of my family now ministers in some capacity or is called to the five-fold ministry. Our children also follow the Lord, and will never know the dark side of demonic possession that their parents once knew.

Even though ignorance of divine revelation may have been prevalent in my grandparent's day, God was still God. He created my family members to be ministers, prophets and apostles, evangelists and teachers, maybe even pastors in the years to come. The enemy saw a family marked by God and attempted to steal, kill and destroy it (John 10:10), but God intervened and caused every one of us to walk in His Kingdom in the pardon of our sin.

So, one whom the enemy desired to pervert into becoming a psychic in his kingdom, was rightfully taken by God to become a prophet of *His* Kingdom. It all happened because of godly roots in grandparents who always confessed to me, "You're going to be somebody in God!" God is stronger than ignorance, just as love is as strong as death (Song of Sol. 8:6), for God is love (1 John 4:16).

May His righteous love blot out every dark corner of your life and that of your loved ones.

Introduction

My purpose in writing this book is to bring about a better understanding of prophets and the prophetic, and to expose misconceptions concerning the office of the prophet. I pray that the reader finishes this book with a broader understanding and a better knowledge of the function of prophets and how to discern between the true and the false.

As one set in the office of prophetess some years ago, I believe the Lord has shown me that this is very much a "prophetic age." All true prophets can attest that the next move of God is pregnant with the prophetic. In fact, everything that is happening as God presses forward into this next move is being preceded by and hinged upon the prophetic.

Some Christians erroneously believe that God has already restored the prophet's office to the Church and is now working on the restoration of the office of the apostle. However, this is not the case. How can the prophet's office have been restored, when most of the Church still has very little understanding of the prophet's ministry, anointing, or calling?

This is the time that God is causing prophets to rise into their true position of authority in the Body and to the world.

We're finally hearing teachings about prophets and apostles that are sensible, true and balanced.

God is establishing and putting the Body of Christ in order. In light of that fact, we should not be dismayed about changes and shifts in the local church as He reorganizes and revamps the structure and foundation. He is just repositioning the "foundation stones," forming and fashioning those called into foundational offices to fit into their appropriate places in the Body.

Still too many Christians are yet void of understanding concerning what a prophet is or what one is called to do. Prophesying is only a fraction of the operation of the prophet. In actuality, prophets are "gifts" (Eph. 4:11,12; 2:20) who help lay foundational doctrines in the Church. They are God's hands extended, articulating His will to the Body.

As a part of the restoration of the prophet to the Body, there must be a proper understanding of the difference between the foundational gift of prophecy and the prophet's office. Many people can flow effectively in the Spirit and dispense a word from God, but prophets supersede fundamentally gifted people with governmental abilities.

There are also the issues of judging prophecy, receiving and dispatching prophecy, and what is the role of prophecy and prophets in this prophetic age.

There's a lot of talk about prophets and prophecy today, but very little real understanding. A few years ago when I first began looking for books concerning my calling, I could not find much on the subject. Today, there are many more good choices available, but I fear, still not enough.

Sadly, the Church as a whole does not have a complete understanding of any of the five-fold offices, much less how they work together. Furthermore, there are just too many Christians who don't even believe that apostles and prophets operate today. But in Ephesians 4, the Apostle Paul wrote that Jesus set five offices in the Body of Christ for a purpose: to perfect the saints and cause them to come into unity in Him. (vv. 12,13.)

It only takes observing your hand to see that you need all five fingers for the hand to operate the way it was created to work. Suppose you lost a finger or two. You can learn to compensate, and you can manage, but your hand will never work as well as it would with all five.

Therefore, how can the Body of Christ be perfected with three "fingers," when Jesus began the work with five? If He had thought three offices could achieve His purpose in the Church, He would have only chosen three. The Holy Spirit is attempting to show us that from the early days of the Church until now, we have been trying, for the most part, to function only as a three-fingered Church.

You may want to ask the question, why is God restoring prophets and apostles in the Church today? The fact of the matter is, they have always been with the Church, but they have not always been recognized for who and what they are. It is my hope that as you conclude reading this book you'll have understanding as to who they are, who they were historically and how it all pertains to you today.

If the Church is to fully carry out the purpose of God in this next century, Christians must stop objecting to the prophets and apostles. They must realize that most objections really stem from their own "doctrines and traditions," and not from the Bible.

God is not writing a new "Bible" in this age. These are not really "new" things He is doing. What God does in every move and every age is to manifest Himself,

His nature and His ways of doing things in what seems to human beings as new ways.

God adapts the things He does to our cultures, our times and our way of understanding and thinking, but His basics do not change.

The Bible says **Jesus Christ is the same yesterday, today, and forever** (Heb. 13:8), and that also applies to God, because Jesus and the Father are one. The purpose of the five-fold offices is to help believers conform corporately to the exact image of Jesus, Who is the exact image of God. (Eph. 4:12,13.) The apostle and prophet play a major part in this scenario as the officers who set the pace for the operation of the entire Body. Their place can no longer be ignored.

I pray that the things God has shown me about prophets, apostles and this "new" prophetic age will add to your understanding of what is happening in the Church today and in the world to come, and that by this knowledge, your life will never be the same.

1
What *Is* a Prophet?

"What is a prophet?" may seem like a ridiculous or unnecessary question to some people. Other people would say that a prophet is someone who foretells the future. However, that is not the "bottom line" of what a prophet is, and we must realize that before we can know the true prophet from the false.

To begin with, a prophet is a *seer,* or one who sees into the supernatural. All prophets are certainly seers, but not all seers are prophets. A *seer's* spiritual eye will show him how God is moving in relation to his area of sight. He may also see the function of a thing as it applies to the Body of Christ. For example, one seer may be anointed by God to *see* into the supernatural as it pertains to the music of a church. He would know by the working of God's Spirit what music would best suit the move of God for the service. Another may function as intercessor to the Body, having insight as to how and when to pray. Prophets have special sight and insight into the governmental aspects of the Church, as well as the function of the members of the Body.

Although a prophet is a person who can foretell future events, this is but one facet or "tool" he uses to fulfill his calling. And not all "prophets" are alike or from God. There are insightful people who are capable of putting trends and events together, predicting a probable outcome, using natural wisdom and intelligence.

There are also worldly prophets who strongly herald some cause or social reform. The Rev. Martin Luther King, Jr. was such a prophet. And there are those who are totally godless, telling of future events by the aid of a familiar spirit, or demon.

But all true prophets are authorized teachers of God's will. They may accomplish this in a variety of ways. However, the important thing to understand is that their teachings are inspired revelations from God and based on His Word.

The most significant thing to know about a real prophet is this:

A prophet is an ordinary person with an extraordinary God working through him or her.

They are not strange "alien beings" walking around as if they've just left the twilight zone! Their actions may seem strange because of their connection to the supernatural.

A prophet is an "oracle" of God, one who articulates what God is saying to individuals, local churches, or the Church at large.

A prophet is a "foundation stone" of the Church, who, along with the apostle, lays foundational doctrines in the Church. (Eph. 2:20.) What does this mean? Quite simply, God has order in His Kingdom. As a part of that order, He has ordained lawyers, so to speak, of the faith who execute and legislate His commands. Apostles and prophets comprise the "holy" supreme court that both expresses and interprets His will. In other words, His prophets see clear pictures in the supernatural and speak what they both see and/or hear to the people.

My first experience with a full-fledged prophet did not occur in a church but in, of all places, a Denny's restaurant! I had only been a Christian for about a year and was out with friends and family members following a revival meeting.

The minister had preached a wonderful message about people who were not fulfilling their purpose in God. Up until that time, I had been insecure about my call to ministry. Even though others had expressed that God's call was assuredly on my life, I was, at the time, too timid and young in spiritual things to accept this. I thought that I was only called to sing, having been trained in opera.

We were sitting around a large table laughing and talking when we noticed a stranger come in. He was seated at a table near ours, ordered his meal, then just dropped his head for a long time and stared down at the floor. Suddenly, he jumped up about three feet from the floor — all six-foot-two of him — and said, "Praise God, I feel the Holy Ghost in here!"

Naturally, everyone turned to look at him, wondering, "Has he lost his mind?" Following this scenario, he came to our table and introduced himself as Tony Marinelli. Then he told us that the Holy Spirit had told him to come to the restaurant. Being a young Christian, I thought that was a peculiar thing for God to do! He looked at each one sitting there, and then knelt at each individual seat, prophesying the Word of the Lord to everyone at that table.

He prophesied such intimate things that I was absolutely astounded. I knew these people very well, and he did not just speak in generalities but told them things no one could know but a few of us who were very close friends and associates.

As he made his way around the table, I was the last one. As it happened, everyone had piled his or her Bible down next to my chair. As that man crouched down beside that pile of Bibles, he pulled my Bible out of the stack! There was no way of knowing which was mine. He laid the Bible beside me and said, "Sister, God says it is not enough for you to sing. You are called to preach the Word of the Lord."

Then he opened my Bible and continued, "The day will come that you will be able to open this Bible, and preach from any page to which it opens. God has placed a tremendous anointing upon you to touch people. You will actually minister to ministers, as well as the general congregation. And you are going to minister around the world."

Needless to say, I lost interest in my meal and everything else! I couldn't even remember what day it was. I would never have believed that something like this was possible.

So you see, his words to me about the future were only a part of his calling as a prophet. He recognized that I was a "lively stone" (1 Pet. 2:5), and God used him to begin to set me in place in the Body. He gave me direction, but you must understand that he did not *call* me. He simply told me that I was called. For me that experience totally destroyed the traditional belief that prophets were not for today.

A wise man once said that a person who has had an experience is never at the mercy of one with an argument against it.

That does not mean that I base my knowledge and understanding of prophets and the prophetic on experience alone. It simply means that I both know and have experienced what the Bible says, and arguments against it have no validity nor credibility.

It was only a short time later that I heard the call of God directly. That particular prophecy prepared me to hear the call. It awakened in me a greater hunger for the things of God. I began seeing visions and having dreams, some of which were very unsettling, and yet strangely exciting. I had no idea what was happening, and there was no one to explain it. I remembered hearing a minister speak about being able to see angels and demons, and remarking to myself how grateful to God I was that I didn't have that gift.

Was I angered when that began to manifest through me! I saw angels and demons as real as the people I see when I speak from the pulpit. This sparked a greater desire to learn about the gifts and about the offices. An intense study ensued, and some seven years later the issue was settled. Finally, I fully accepted the call as a prophet, and one man's obedience helped pull me into destiny.

Prophecy, Prophets and the Gift of Prophecy

What is prophecy? It is the "act of foretelling or forthtelling" events that have not yet happened. However, the two different operations of a prophet and the "gift of prophecy" are often confused one with another.

Someone who manifests the gift of prophecy should have a very strong prophetic flow that stems out of an astute relationship with God. Anyone who is born again and filled with the Holy Spirit can potentially flow in the gift of prophecy, but of course, all don't.

Paul wrote about the gift of prophecy in his first letter to the Christians at Corinth, who were apparently having difficulty in knowing how to allow the Holy Spirit's gifts to manifest in an orderly fashion:

> **But he who prophesies speaks edification and exhortation and comfort to men.**
>
> **He who speaks in a tongue edifies himself, but he who prophesies edifies the church.**
>
> **1 Corinthians 14:3,4**

Paul thought the gift of prophecy so important that he would rather they prophesied than that they spoke in tongues, although he wrote that he spoke in tongues more than all of them. (1 Cor. 14:18.)

Those who operate in a gift of prophecy do not have as heavy a responsibility as those who are set in the office of prophet. However, there still are guidelines to be followed, as Paul wrote to the Corinthians. If you operate in the gift of prophecy, I would suggest studying 1 Corinthians 12-14 for revelation from the Holy Spirit concerning this gift and its operation.

A rule of thumb: Prophecy should never be given to anyone when there is no one else to witness, write down, or record it. There are few exceptions to this rule. This not only protects the one who receives the word, but it protects the giver. This is just as important for prophets as it is for those who operate in the gift of prophecy. Unfortunately, for the most part, people hear what they want to hear, or they interpret something a prophet says according to their own understanding of the words. Often what they come up with is not correct. Having the exact words written down or recorded will save you much trouble and possible heartache.

So never give what I call "parking lot" prophecies if it can be avoided. **The spirits of the "prophets" are subject to the prophets** (1 Cor. 14:32). That means you can wait until there is someone to judge. If you are really operating in the gift of prophecy or office of prophet, you will not mind having your words judged, being grateful for a confirmation, affirmation of accuracy, or even correction. Also, it is equally important to understand who is actually capable of judging prophecy. First Corinthians 14:29 says, **Let two or three prophets speak, and let the others judge,** which more than implies seasoned operators in the prophetic and not merely someone who flows.

No one should ever attempt to operate prophetically in the local church without the pastor or ministry head's express consent or direction. There are no universal prophets or apostles, which means God does not give you permission to walk into just anyone's church and prophesy. The Holy Spirit, Who testifies of Jesus (Rev. 19:10), always follows God's order. If you are really sent by God, you will be recognized by the eldership and chief shepherd of the church, which validates your word to the people.

After following proper protocol and gaining permission, wait on God for the correct time to release the word. I guarantee you will not burst at the seams as some think, but everyone will be edified by your obedience. Prophecy will often confirm what is being preached, affirming what God desires to say to the people. Since the Holy Spirit never interrupts Himself, you can expect an undisruptive flow.

Whether operating in the gift or the office, just know that there will be times when mistakes will be made, especially when you first begin. The Prophet Samuel is the only one I'm aware of, even in the Bible, to whom the Lord said He would **let none of his words fall to the ground** (1 Sam. 3:19). Samuel never missed it prophetically. In other words, God backed up every prophesy he spoke. However, this says to us that some prophet's words could fall to the ground even though they are true prophets. We'll examine this further later in the book.

The grace gifts of God are given to every believer to enhance their ability to walk in a certain level of authority in the earth. In fact, the authority of the believer is pretty powerful. Just by coming into covenant with God through the blood of Jesus, your authority becomes far greater than the power of the enemy, Satan. The tragedy is, not every believer is aware of his, or her, potential, allowing Satan to keep them from walking in that authority. Therefore, God's prophets must not only grow to understand that potential, but allow it to flow through them, teaching others how to totally disarm the enemy.

In his letter to the Ephesians, Paul wrote about the office of the prophet:

> **And He Himself gave some to be apostles, some prophets, some evangelists, and some pastors and teachers.**
>
> **Ephesians 4:11**

In that same chapter, we see that one purpose of the prophet's office is to perfect the saints for the work of the ministry, and to edify the Body. Prophets also are to work in conjunction with the other five-fold offices to bring the Body of Christ into the unity of the faith and purpose and into the knowledge of God's will. There are a number of ways through which that can be accomplished. In the next chapter, I will discuss them more fully as we explore the office of the prophet.

The basic difference between a prophet and someone who manifests the gift of prophecy is precisely what Paul wrote to the Ephesians:

1. A prophet is one of the five "governing" positions set in the Church by God. He has authority in the Body of Christ that someone who simply operates in the gift of prophecy does not have.

2. The gift of prophecy is not given as a governmental office but to comfort, exhort and edify the Body of Christ. It flows deeply from the Holy Spirit but does not govern. In Romans 12:6, Paul calls this gift one of the "grace gifts," something given through the grace of God for the benefit of His Church.

Paul wrote in the same chapter that every believer has a gift or function in the Body that creates unity and makes the Body work. Obviously, every believer is not to govern in the Church or we would have chaos and anarchy.

A mature prophet should be able to have all of the nine gifts (or more accurately defined, manifestations) of the Holy Spirit (spoken of in 1 Cor. 12:8-10) flowing through him. If you enjoy a consecrated life and spend much time on your face before God, you will function in the deep flow of God. This should be the true source of these manifestations, or the flow will be shallow or soulish.

Before I was called to the office of prophet, I walked first in the gift of prophecy. When I received the call to ministry, I was washing dishes at my kitchen sink, quietly talking to the Lord. Suddenly, I found myself sprawled across the kitchen floor! When I arose, the Holy Spirit began to speak to me concerning a call, first to evangelism, after which another ministry would follow. He told me that I would literally travel the world bringing the Word of God to the nations.

At first, that was difficult for me to accept. I did not feel I was capable of fulfilling this demand upon my life. So God knew He could not tell me at that time that eventually I would be called as a prophetess. However, He did what He could do, and that was to stir up the foundational gift of prophecy within me. It began by my seeing "pictures" (visions) which came to pass.

In Revelation 19:10, we see that **the testimony of Jesus is the spirit of prophecy.** Therefore, if Jesus is within you and you are *in* Him, the potential for the gift of prophecy is already resident within you. But just because that gift is stirred in you does not mean that you are called as a prophet.

Many people have operated in the gift of prophecy and thus assume they are prophets. Aptly, these misguided ones cause a lot of confusion in the Body concerning the prophetic. Not being called as prophets, they sometimes "prophesy" out of their souls or direct people out of their own desires. If they keep "aspiring" for the prophet's anointing to which God has not called them, they may eventually fall prey to a "familiar spirit," a counterfeit spirit from the enemy. This spirit can only mimic the true and can be discerned by its generalities or familiarity with carnal things alone.

After studying prophets and prophecy for many years, and knowing intimately many who stand in the office, as well as operating in the office myself, I have come to believe that these gifts are placed in us as we are formed in the womb, and not at the "new" birth.

When you are born again, these often dormant gifts are stirred by God. Then you must be brought into maturity and trained in the operation of those gifts. The same is true of a call to any office. Some people actually operate in the supernatural before salvation, having these once dormant gifts operational by and through the kingdom of darkness. They enter into the prophetic illegally, or under an "unholy" anointing. Some do it knowingly as satanic witches, or unknowingly as authentic psychics or mediums. But the Bible makes it painfully clear that Christians are not to operate in, nor seek the counsel, of such people.

Therefore, there is no substitute for getting into the Bible daily or for developing a strong prayer life and relationship with God. If you are not in a position to have your spirit cleansed daily by the washing of water by the Word (Eph. 5:26), you will be oblivious to the supernatural things of God and open to the entrance of familiar spirits.

What Is a Familiar Spirit?

The basic difference between the Holy Spirit and that of a familiar spirit is the way in which this demonic spirit operates. It tells you things that are *familiar* concerning the past or present, or knowledge of a familiar, carnal nature concerning previous generations. It can also predict some future events but cannot tell you anything from the Kingdom of light. The Bible clearly states that the kingdom of darkness cannot comprehend (understand or interpret) the Kingdom of light. (John 1:5.)

Demons, or evil spirits, apparently have been here since before man was on the earth. Familiar spirits have been around you and your ancestors long enough to know you personally. They probably were assigned to your family line and have familiarized themselves with those characteristics. These spirits know what sins were committed that have not been repented of and placed under the blood. They also know what consequences they can legally inflict upon your descendants. This is what is called "a generational curse."

A familiar spirit, as well as God's Spirit, knows if you are open to the supernatural or closed to it. It is clearly possible for a person to be born "open," I believe, because someone in their near lineage knowingly operated as a medium or "psychic," or ultimately as a holy prophet. A familiar spirit might be able to predict accurately what you will do or how you will react based on that knowledge. They are also capable of predicting some future events planned in the kingdom of darkness, such as the bombing of the World Trade Center. Likewise, the Holy Spirit, Who has knowledge of all things, knows how to bring you to the point of accountability and salvation to manifest a true prophetic anointing.

Prophecies of destructive future events given by persons which operate by familiar spirits do not have to come to pass. We can stop the enemy's plans by coming against him with the Word of God and doing warfare in the spirit.

If you have ever read any articles containing predictions by "tabloid fortune tellers," you know that their track record is not very good. Their rate of accuracy is frightfully low, particularly considering how many people are following them. In the lives of individuals, the accuracy rate only increases, statistically, by a narrow margin. So why is there seemingly so much curiosity concerning this psychic phenomenon? Quite simply because people are looking for answers concerning the supernatural without accountability to God.

The incredible truth is, psychics are more often wrong than right, leading us to believe that the majority of psychics, card and palm readers and fortune tellers are not even operating under familiar spirits, but are absolute fakes! They are in it for the money and the popularity.

Still, the world is operating under the false conception that this is a "pyschic" age, instead of understanding that this is really a *prophetic* age. No one will ever find lasting truth about the supernatural without first finding the truth about Jesus Christ.

The world is defining prophetic as psychic and accepting anyone who prophesies or represents himself as being able to know the future as a "prophet." This is a very dangerous misconception that is opening up literally millions to the influence or actual possession of demons. "Psychic hotlines" have increased this potential by leaps and bounds, and, unbelievably so, even many Christians are accepting these people as valid.

Popular Misconceptions

In addition, there are several common misconceptions about the prophetic that more than a few Christians have who *do* know the difference between the psychic and the prophetic but are misinformed about the prophetic.

Perhaps the most common misconception about prophets is that *if their prophecies fail* according to men's standards, they are not true prophets. I want Christians to understand that prophets are human and not infallible. There is at least one instance in Scripture of a true prophet of God whose prophecy did not come to pass. Likewise, there was a reason why.

1. The Prophet Jonah was sent by God to prophesy that judgment would fall on the city of Nineveh, the capital of Assyria, in forty days — but it did not happen! (Jonah 3:4.) Why did this not come true? The people of Nineveh heeded Jonah's prophetic preaching

and repented. Many prophecies from God are His merciful attempts to give people an opportunity to repent so that He will not have to bring hard judgment. This is a wonderful example of a prophecy of God's judgment being averted for hundreds of years due to true repentance and intercession.

In other words, there are *conditional* prophecies, or words that will come true *if* a person obeys what is foretold. Jonah was not a false prophet because his word from God did not happen within the forty days. Jonah's prophecy was fulfilled dramatically after Jonah's lifetime when Nineveh once again turned away from God.

2. It is quite possible for true prophets to miss God. Assuredly, no one but Jesus is perfect, but we all are being perfected. (Eph. 4:12.) Perhaps a prophet may misinterpret what he or she hears from God, or may miss God's timing. It is not likely that a true prophet will miss God if he or she is really flowing with the Lord, but it is possible.

I'm sure that the critics of Jonah's day attempted to label him a false prophet, but the truth of the matter is, he knew God's mercy and expected the outcome. His own prejudice caused him to miss the importance of his mission. He failed to recognize the sovereignty of God and the fact that God alone gives the prophecy or it is false! In other words, it took God to make Jonah the prophet he was.

3. Another interesting example of a prophet who obviously was a true prophet but whose word failed is found in Numbers 33:7-13. God's original word to Moses was that he would lead the children of Israel into the promised land. But because Moses smote the rock instead of speaking to it, God indicted him, charging that he could not go into the promised land. Further, Moses

changed God's word to Israel, saying, "Must we fetch you water out of the rock?" instead of simply performing God's original word to him. His anger caused him to disobey, and thus lose access to the blessing. Nonetheless, this failure did not cause Moses to be listed among the false prophets. Despite his humanness, Moses is the only prophet with whom God Himself said He met face to face.

Another rank misconception about prophets is that the prophet should interpret words of personal prophecy to individuals and make them absolutely clear. It has been my experience as a prophet that prophets either *cannot* or *should not* interpret a prophetic word, and neither should the person receiving it!

Of course, this should not be confused with a prophet's God-given intuitive ability to *comprehend* what God is saying. It applies in principle to a prophet's filtering God's words through his own *perceptions* alone. He may perceive correctly or incorrectly. For example, God may express to Rev. Jones that He desires a humble heart, meaning He requires a place of humility not yet obtained by the minister. But the prophet may perceive God means that He desires that minister subject himself to humiliation. If the prophet acts upon what is rightly comprehended of God, and not his natural or theological perceptions, the minister will be correctly edified.

My husband George and I receive many prophetic words. We have found that most of the time, those prophecies would turn out to be *similar* to what we initially thought, but almost never *exactly* what we perceived them to be. Further, the time frame of manifestation was seldom precisely with what we thought it would be.

This is why with my personal ministry, George and I insist on having prophecies either written or recorded. This encompasses prophecies I give and ones we receive. It protects the prophet as well as the receiver. It also clarifies for the recipient whether the word is conditional and may require some act of obedience to cause it to come to pass. If God is gracious and kind enough to say it, we ought to be sensitive and gracious enough to listen to precisely what He said and not rely upon our fallible memory.

A third misconception is that prophecy is always for the immediate future. Prophetic words are generally seasonal, and you must wait for the season of their fulfillment. Furthermore, prophets being in the presence of a timeless God may speak of a thing as though it is now, when actually it is many years away.

A fourth misconception is that all prophets are to operate alike, or function under the same anointing (unction). Most prophecies that I have personally given to individuals begin in their past, cover their present and draw them into the future. I know other prophets who begin with the present, and yet others who go straight to the future, when another may start in the past and jump to the future.

Nor do all prophets prophesy in the same style. I have observed some who actually prophesy in "rap," some whose words rhyme poetically, some who still use the "thus saith the Lord" form, and others who speak in a conversational manner.

A fifth is a noted misconception, and that is that God will not embarrass you. It may be truer to say the Spirit will not embarrass you for the fun of it, which would be cruel or *unnecessary.* However, if He must shake you for your own good, He will. Perhaps there is a need to make you face a reality that is destroying your life, your ministry, or even your salvation. Do not think for a moment that He is more concerned about temporarily embarrassing you than about life and death matters!

Jude 23 talks about saving some from the fire through fear. This means that God will openly rebuke you if there is no other way He can get your attention. However, it is unusual for God to send a person operating merely in the gift of prophecy with a strong rebuke, for He would rather entrust it to a seasoned prophet. Gifts of prophecy, or grace gifts, are used to edify, comfort and exhort. They build up the Body.

Rebukes, when they do come, usually are very stern, strong and straight-forward. They tear down wrong doctrines, behavior, attitudes and falsehoods. Remember, when God tears down, He reconstructs or replaces, and if it remains destroyed, He never intended it to be at all. In those instances, He will display His ultimate intention. An excellent example is found in Matthew 23:37. **O Jerusalem, Jerusalem, the one who kills the prophets and stones those who are sent to her! How often I wanted to gather your children together, as a hen gathers her chicks under her wings, but you were not willing!**

From that point He continues by prophesying judgment, foretelling the desolation of Jerusalem, destroying with His words every false regime. Jesus literally tore down their present power structures, leaving them with a weighty conditional word of deliverance. **You shall not see Me until the time comes when you say, "Blessed is He who comes in the name of the Lord!"** (Luke 13:35).

Jesus is our perfect example as the prophet of all prophets. He sets the stage for literally every attribute and ability of the New Testament prophet. For those who would argue that New Testament prophets cannot bring judgment, look to our example, **for the testimony of Jesus is the spirit of prophecy** (Rev. 19:10).

Jesus set the tone for every believer who would ever flow in the supernatural in any capacity, and opened the door for the greatest deliverance of all — deliverance from spiritual death. We no longer have to fall prey to seducing, familiar spirits or lying psychic phenomenon but we can know the truth and be free to explore this prophetic age.

2

What Is the True Call of a Prophet?

As foundational gifts to the Church, the true call of the prophet is not just to tell people of the future. Prophecy is invariably the Word of God spoken with power to tear down and reconstruct, to edify, comfort and exhort, to articulate the will of God to the people, and to bring us to intercession on behalf of people, churches and nations. This may be accomplished by preaching and teaching as well as prognostication.

It is very important that a foundation of prayer and intercession become an integral part of prophetic ministry. A prophet will not have much revelation if he is not willing to give God time in intercession and prayer. He must be willing to travail and cry out to God for those to whom he is sent.

Each time God sends me among new people, I seek Him for how He desires to flow among them. If I have not interceded for them, I will not be as effective in depth or accuracy in the prophetic.

Perhaps my prayer life is different from the average Christian. I do not structure my day with blocks of time for prayer. Instead, I rise praying and continue to talk to God all through the day. Of course, I do set special times to get in secret with Him for specific needs, both for myself and especially for others. But basically, I try to stay in a place of continual prayerful communication with the Father.

One of the strongest bits of advice for budding prophets, or anyone called to prophetic ministry, is to develop an active prayer life. Prayer and study of the Word are basic necessities for a consecrated, meaningful life. Living a consecrated life also means watching the words that proceed from your mouth even when you are not operating prophetically. You must not allow bitterness, anguish, or evil to reign in your heart, lest they come out of your mouth when prophesying.

A true prophet must impact lives in a peculiar way. He must be bold enough to deliver rebukes, but compassionate enough not to destroy the person. He must also be sensitive enough to detect hurts and withdrawal. Prophets must discern each "lively stone," and their place of fitting that no one feels neglected by God or the Church.

Every prophet must be purged in order to live a consecrated, holy life, and that is never fun. However, the correction or cleansing of the Lord reaps the peaceable fruit of righteousness. Nonetheless, I would never, ever have called myself to such a ministry! In fact, twenty years ago I would not have believed I would be doing this today. After receiving the call to minister, it took three years for the prophetic to soundly manifest, but another five years to accept the call as a prophetess. But just as the Scriptures affirm, men began to confirm my call, ordaining and commissioning me to that purpose.

Now, I could not imagine myself doing anything else! In fact, I do not know a prophet who would have elected to become one. God takes you through tremendous paces to build and develop your character. Many times, it seems that God absolutely hides His face from us in order to cause us to press in deeper to Him. It seems that in those times He will not speak to or through us, nor look at us. He'll do nothing for us — except increase our hunger for Him. And, if we are not willing to persevere in faith and prayer during those dry seasons, we will not see Him as He desires us to see Him.

There comes for prophets seasons of deep introspective looks into our own hearts. Everything that is not pleasing to God in those seasons is relinquished to Him for cleansing. It's not always pleasant when God begins housecleaning. In fact, my lifestyle is one of constantly checking every area, making sure I am in right standing with God and man. I sense better than anyone else if I'm off base, for I could wreak havoc in the lives of those to whom I minister. A prophet out of alignment with God can destroy the very thing he was sent to build.

If I am making it sound as if the prophet's office and anointing is one of hardship, it is not my intention. However, I do intend for you to know that you must go through something to fulfill that office. From your early years on, if you are called as a prophet, you will go through critical, strenuous moldings and shapings, "sandpapering" away rough edges. But the finished product is a tapestry, a work of art wrought by the hand of God Himself.

My first year as a Christian, I studied the Bible with my mother for five solid months, day and night. At the end of that five months, I had the first divine healing of my life. I was healed of a deathly illness. My mother also was delivered from several critical ailments and received her divine call.

I was born again right in the middle of the Word of Faith movement. In fact, I was "Miss Word of Faith" herself! If I had not grasped the teachings of Kenneth

Hagin, Kenneth Copeland, Fred Price and others, I would not have lived to see this day. Within an eleven-year period, I have been terminally ill three times, and nearly wiped out in an accident once. I have learned through my experience how to endure hardness as a good soldier. But there are Christians today — even spiritual leaders — who want to avoid the word *suffering* altogether.

Somehow they want us to think that all suffering comes from the devil. If we suffer in any way, they say we lack faith, or have done something wrong, even quoting the scripture, **A curse without cause shall not alight** (Prov. 26:2). These people do not believe that God also tests us and that He never promised to keep us *from* all trials and tribulations, but He promised to walk through with us. (Isa. 43:2.)

I found that suffering builds great character, and that if you are going to walk in the office of prophet, you are going to suffer to get there. I went through some unique sufferings. But the ridicule, rejection, harsh rebukes, yes, even defeats, only served to build in me an unshakable faith in God's sovereignty and faithfulness. If I had not developed this fortitude, I would not be able to skillfully administer my office

All of that was to develop an "Esther." When she was chosen to appear before the king as a potential queen, Esther went to the head of the king's harem, and asked him to pick what she should wear — even perfume and cosmetics — and show her what to do that would please the king. By doing so, she became queen and saved her people from genocide. (See the book of Esther.)

In studying this story in the Bible, I determined to go before the Holy Spirit and ask Him to show me how to please *my* King, Jesus. That led me to understand that a prophet must have the kind of temperament to take correction, reproof, suffering and testing in order to stand before and beside the King of kings.

Change Begins With Accepting the Call

Many people have written to me or have asked me in person how to know the true call of a prophet. They earnestly request guidelines to show them the difference between being called to the office or simply operating in the grace gift of prophecy. Usually I begin by sharing my testimony of being called.

God took me an unusual route around the mountain, so to speak, to get to this point in my life. When I seriously answered the call to ministry, I had no doubt that the call was genuine. My actions were much like Elisha's when he was called by Elijah. (1 Kings 19. I went to all of my teachers and colleagues in the operatic field, bidding them a fond adieu.

You can imagine their reactions. I was attending a secular institution, one of the top ten universities in the country for music. Their financial investment in me, up to this point, had been heavy and was geared toward developing a star who would attract quality students from around the world.

I had built an excellent reputation in undergraduate school. The graduate school expected the same thing. You can imagine their consternation when I decided to go into the ministry. This was not the return they expected on their investment. It was difficult for them to believe there was a legitimate call of God on my life considering what a "hellion" I had been!

These unbelievers looked upon me as being temporarily insane, and believed I would soon return to my right mind. In 1994, it has been sixteen years, and I still have not returned to my "right mind," and I never will by the world's standards.

This unusual route proved to be the way that I would go in God's estimation. Theater taught me how to be sensitive to those around me and how to endure hard, rigid criticism without losing focus. It developed a keen sense of timing and the theatrical antics that often accompany a demonstrative prophet's ministry. In view of this, it is not strange at all that God chose that route to develop the singer who became prophet.

Prophets are not normally God's "social butterflies." They love people, but feel the internal need to be secluded from them in order to better serve them. This is much the same attribute of a well-studied actor who prepares his artistry alone and is brilliant on stage. Therefore, an intense study of the Word is mandatory for everyone flowing in the prophetic. It is out of the depth of knowledge you have of God by His Word that you are called. But if you don't know His Word, you won't recognize His voice calling, for He only speaks in conjunction with His Word.

Twenty Tests of a Prophet

As part of my answer to those requesting how to recognize the call, I want to share an excerpt from a book by my friend, Paula Price, called, *Constructing the Contemporary Prophet,* a comprehensive "crash course" in the prophet's mantle. (*Constructing the Contemporary Prophet* is available through Vincom Publishers and Distributors.)

1. **A propensity toward having dreams and visions.** While everyone dreams, prophets seem to have more than their share, each dream having very wide

dimensions. He is forced to do more with them than acknowledge having had them.

2. **A sensitivity to spiritual things.** Prophets have a natural curiosity and longing for the things of the Spirit. From their earliest recollections, prophets can remember supernatural encounters. They are highly intuitive, incisive, perceptive and pensive, probing the dark secret side of things.

3. **A comprehension of prophetic matters.** Prophets comprehend prophetic matters even if it is acquired from external, non-religious circumstances. God fine tunes it, since it becomes a prophetic endowment.

4. **An understanding of the place of prophecy in the Body.** The prophet perceives early the powerful forces that drive and govern the natural world. Prophecy becomes a detail of that supernatural government when communicating to men.

5. **An awareness of Jesus as the Spirit of prophecy**. True prophets realize that apart from Jesus, prophecy is erroneous. It must symphathize and identify with Christ totally. The prophet must strive to remain within the confines of God's truth in order to accurately disperse His Word.

6. **Peculiar or unusual interpretative skills.** Explaining the spiritual and supernatural undertones of matters with sound grounded wisdom. Prophets deal with abstract principles that must be articulated in normal terminology to the Body.

7. **A capacity for revelation discovery.** Prophets must be able to accurately, potently uncover truth, disclosing what is really from God's Word and illuminate it to mankind.

8. **An extraordinary wisdom and insight.** Prophets cannot counsel according to soulish wisdom, but

godly. They have an innate ability to identify problems often overthrowing heretical solutions.

9. **A great sense of the application of prophecy.** This is the bedrock of effective counseling. Prophets know where, when and how to flow.

10. **A heightened spiritual discernment, a keen perception of the spiritual world, and an easy detection of the instigations of spiritual forces.** Prophets discern how the enemy is working against people, ministering deliverance and freedom.

11. **An inordinate grasp of the Scriptures.** Scriptures play the dominant role in the prophetic ministry. They become the basis by which all aspects of the ministry are judged. They must exhibit an inexplicable grasp of the Word. Studying the Bible for them is studying culture, history, government and purpose. They must have a superb understanding of the Word to execute these abilities. This call is always preceded by a deep hunger for knowledge of God.

12. **A potential for inspired utterances.** That is the capacity for accurately communicating messages from the supernatural Kingdom of God. This becomes a keystone for realizing the true call from prophetic outbursts that come true, consistently and accurately, over a period of time.

13. **A remarkable accuracy in divine communication.** This asset is self-explanatory. An uncanny ability to draw from the supernatural with exactness.

14. **Governmental abilities.** There *are* ranks of prophets. Some are called to local bodies as "house" prophets, some to nations, some to the Church, others to the secular, and so forth. Still other prophets are called to establish powerful works, teaching the Word of the

Lord to their generation. Government involves legislation, emitment, influence, discipline, restraint, enforcement and punishment. This carries a heavy weight of responsibility. They must apprehend God's standards and reinforce them in the Church, especially the call to holiness.

15. **Strong literary skills.** Those who are called and matured to higher ranks have the responsibility of leaving something written in the earth for future generations to read.

This kind of prophetic calling requires some education. A prophet of this order must have the ability to coherently put his or her thoughts on paper in a form that could be read by readers of any level of education. You need not be a Rhodes scholar or have any number of college degrees, but you must be literate enough to communicate effectively in writing. This order of prophets must also exhibit strong analytical skills, or the ability to read someone else's work and discern how true, accurate or scripturally correct it is.

16. **Impressive elocution or an authority manifesting in your speech that arrests people in their tracks, causing them to hear by the Spirit.** Prophets are persuasive and engaging speakers. Although perfect grammar may not be evident, their speech evidences conviction.

Forcing people to listen through sheer volume or a commanding personality is not the sign of a prophet, even though they may exhibit these qualities. Instead, knowledge, wisdom, humor, humility and integrity with clarity are elocution strengths.

17. **An unusual "judicial" aptitude, which means prudence, perception and integrity.** Being a chief

officer of the Church, a prophet will have to exercise judicial insight most of the time. Prudence, shrewdness and perception, as well as integrity, calm and objectivity, are God's "professional" prophetic endowments. Rashness, haste and instability, as well as lack of fairness, defeat the work. These qualities come by rich life experiences, overcoming obstacles while remaining consistently in faith.

If you are called to an office, you will be accountable before God at the Judgment for what you did with that office, whether you ever answered the call and operated in it or not. If a prophet loses his anointing through carnal sin, greed, pride and worldly ambition, or other sins, his calling remains. This opens a door for the demonic perversion of the gift, creating a false prophet from what perhaps began as a true prophet.

The Bible records in the book of Numbers that Balaam was such an example. Greed and ambition eventually destroyed him. Integrity is the prophet's meat and drink, for he realizes he is first judged by the standard of God's judgment by which He rules.

18. **A fierce allegiance and obedience to God and to the things of God.** There must be total commitment to God's holiness, consecrated demeanor, truth and righteousness.

Allegiance to God is also respect and allegiance to His people and authorities. Prophets must not circumvent the leadership of the church, but must submit to some. With grave and earnest intensity and maturity, they must pursue the will of God and the execution of their office while exercising great restraint. The prophet must always recognize he is merely a servant.

19. **Judicial aptitude and organizational abilities, or executive or administrative talents pertaining to the**

Church. This means having the ability to see how things fit together, setting the order of the organism which is the Church.

This also includes outstanding leadership ability and an instinct for gathering and guiding people. Prophets strong in the Lord are forceful, gifted visionaries who influence churches and people. They are determined, self-starters, self-motivators with strong initiatives.

Foundations, principles, procedures, methods and standards, and implementation guidelines are very important to prophetic ministry. Prophets should be able to "call" and identify ministries, setting in position the lively stones which comprise the Body. This unique sensitivity also allows the prophet to predict how, when and where God is moving.

20. **Outstanding leadership abilities.** This addresses the native instinct for overseeing, to the end, a specific purpose or goal. It speaks to an inherent capacity to influence, regulate and control human behavior.

This does not allow the prophet to be manipulative or controlling, which is abusive. It does promote no nonsense, perseverance and dedication.

These twenty capabilities leave no room for inconsistent, unscriptural, intolerable behavior. Prophets must remain within these ramifications.

I have heard of so-called "prophets" and "apostles" who have entered local churches dictating to pastors, executing a false, corrupt, manipulative attitude. This is, I believe, an abomination to God. There are no universal prophets or apostles. All must observe the authorities of God's house and His laws. These twenty characteristics are meant to serve as guidelines, whether you are called to an office or to operate in the gift of prophecy. They were created also to help you discern between the true and the false prophet.

If the vast majority of these traits are not already evident in your life to some extent, perhaps this is an indication that you are not called to the office of prophet. Of course, there is also the possibility that they may as yet be undeveloped.

Surely God will confirm your call by the evidence of these traits as well as the affirming words of other prophets and ministers. Not everyone can see themselves and their own abilities clearly. And in whatever position you find yourself in relation to the prophetic, be glad, realizing that God's wisdom supersedes that of man's, and He will guide you into great fulfillment.

3

The Role of Prophet in the Five-Fold Ministry

When I began to study the Church in relation to the prophetic, I found it to be "lopsided." In addition to trying to accomplish its purpose with three offices instead of the full complement of five established by Jesus, the Church is like a horse with a bruised nose from pushing a cart, instead of pulling it with a team.

We have erroneously thought that ministry gifts are people the believers invest in to do the work of the ministry that Jesus really called them to do! Jesus told believers to take the Gospel to the whole world, and He told the five-fold offices to train or equip them to fulfill the call. (Eph. 4:11,12.)

Instead, believers think they are to sit in pews and financially support the five-fold offices' efforts to win the world to Jesus. And, even in financial support, believers have not done their part. About 20 percent of Christians tithe and support all of the works of the Church. The other 80 percent are riding on the good graces of the 20 percent.

The Lord said something to me once that is so profound. He said, "Don't you dare send your money to anyone else, expecting them to do what I told you to do. Instead, faithfully, financially support the work of others as their work and your work as your own."

I once asked God, "Why aren't we seeing signs, wonders and miracles as we have in other movements?"

He said very pointedly, "I poured out My Spirit abroad upon certain individuals to show My people that common, ordinary, everyday people could stand under an extraordinary anointing. Believers could be used mightily by Me, even though some of them are not even called as five-fold ministry gifts."

Many may argue this point, but Kathryn Kuhlman always insisted that she was not called to any of the five-fold offices, but simply as a believer whom God used as He willed. Yet, more signs, wonders and genuine miracles took place in her meetings than in almost any other modern Christian figure.

God does this to show us how He desires to move by His Spirit and to attract millions to come into the fullness of the Church. Instead, the Church unfairly idolizes and exalts the people God uses, causing a misconception that five-fold ministers alone are called to service.

We began to think the five-fold ministry was to do all of the work, especially a small group of "special" stars. The remaining members of this Body are to sit and wait for them to perform to their critical satisfaction. Just as significant, the Lord expressed a further reason for the diminishing of miracles is that the apostle and prophet are not in their proper place. Both show a propensity toward signs, wonders and miracles as a mark of the call, particularly during times of transition in the Body.

The biblical truth is that *everyone is called to serve God in some capacity.* Each believer has a definite purpose in this day and age. The ultimate call of the prophetic ministry today is to finally draw and place people into their rightful position and purpose.

Prophets Are To Lay Foundations

Prophets are a foundation gift in the Body of Christ, according to Ephesians 2:20:

> **Having been built on the foundation of the apostles and prophets, Jesus Christ Himself being the chief cornerstone.**

That means, specifically, that God has sent His Word into the earth, and God intends for His Word to be fulfilled. He uses the prophet and the apostle as His mouthpiece and implementer to establish His Word in the Church.

Prophet Mark Chironna of Raleigh, NC, has said, "The prophet sees, drawing up the blueprint, and the apostle sees and constructs the building according to the blueprint."

That is the simplest way I have heard to explain the functioning of the apostle and the prophet. The apostle cannot function without the prophet, and the prophet surely cannot function without the apostle. As a matter of fact, an apostle will have, at some point in his training, walked in all of the five-fold ministry offices: apostle, prophet, evangelist, pastor and teacher. He is described as the minister that wears all five hats.

In addition, every true prophet also will have a teacher's mantle and somewhat of a pastor's heart. A prophet without the compassionate side of a pastor's heart would have no compassion or mercy when delivering a rebuke. He would be likely to tear down and never rebuild, and (at times) gleefully slay sheep.

It is imperative in this prophetic age that the five-fold ministries operate by God's order. We should consider it a privilege to be chosen to serve God in any capacity. Be grateful to God for what you are called to do, and not call yourself to a ministry that seems prestigious or important.

Consider this: If someone calls himself to an office he must also anoint himself to fulfill that office, because God will not. And, eventually, he will stand before God and give an account for why he tried to walk in an office to which he was not called, consequently neglecting something to which he probably was called.

If you are meant to be a "hand," and you try to function as a foot, you will cripple and minimize your function, dwarfing your potential. God will judge you both by the error of attempting to be a foot and what was left undone since you are actually a hand.

The five-fold offices were given by Jesus to bring the Church into a common unity of purpose in Him. (Eph. 4:13.) They are not to be in competition or to operate out of jealousy. Because the apostle is a composite of the other four, he is the highest ranking of the five offices.

However, that does not mean the apostle is more important to God, or more superior as a person or as a Christian. Neither is he the head of the Body, but he is a higher authority in his function with great responsibility.

The prophet, like the apostle, can give direction to the Church. In some circles today, it is believed that a New Testament prophet cannot give direction. It is also believed that there is no need for a great number of prophets to a generation or for a prophet to be appointed in each local body. God may not have a prophet stationary in each body, but He makes provision for one to have a voice in each.

The Bible does not say anywhere that prophets were eliminated. Nor does the Bible say that, because Jesus came to earth, died and rose again to sit at the right hand of God, He no longer needs "mouthpieces" in the earth. It does say, specifically, that Jesus Himself ordained the five-fold offices, not just to establish the early Church, but to minister His grace to every generation until He returns.

Prophets draw attention to Jesus, giving Him honor, and seeing to it that He gets all of the glory due Him. Any prophet who does not venerate Jesus is probably not one to whom you ought to listen. Like the prophet, John the Baptist, we must decrease in order for Jesus to increase. (John 3:30.)

All of the offices, like the Holy Spirit, are to draw attention to Jesus and to hold Him up before the world. This is also the mandate of the Body, whose potential we have not reached.

Prophets, most certainly, can give steering and direction. Anything you see the prophets in the Old Testament do, is "legal" for the prophets in the New Testament.

God Will Let Us Know If He Changes Things

Texas teacher-pastor Rick Godwin says it this way: If a concept is mentioned in the Old Testament and you do not see it again in the New Testament, it does not mean it was done away with. It means that God did *not* change it!

If God changed something or did away with it, He would have told us. Old Testament things either were done away with and replaced, changed, or remain the same.

How do you know the difference? You "pass it by the cross." For example, animal sacrifices were totally done away with, because Jesus became the eternal sacrificial Lamb of God. This is confirmed through the book of Hebrews as well as the entire New Testament.

If it was done away with or changed, God told us in the New Testament.

If He did not mention it in the New Testament, it was not changed. Somehow some teachers have inverted this concept to say that it *was* done away with if it was not mentioned.

For example, there are people who say we do not need to tithe because that is part of the Old Testament covenant. However, in the New Testament, it is just as important to give tithes and offerings as ever before, for now it is an act of the heart. God now circumcises the heart, not the flesh. And God did not tell us tithing was done away with.

Dancing before the Lord is not mentioned in the New Testament. Therefore, God did not change it. He should not have to tell us that we are permitted and encouraged to dance before Him. His people have always included dance as part of their worship and praise.

A prophet's ministry lays a foundation for the Church. By revelation, a prophet interprets Scripture and teaches the Body what God is saying. They also "forthtell" and show the Church by revelation how God is moving at a particular time.

Prophecy is a very viable and necessary force in the Body, particularly in this new move of God.

The Apostle Paul, who operated in a strong prophetic flow and also was a prophet, evangelist, pastor and teacher, rebuked the churches to which he wrote emphatically. Immediately behind each rebuke, however, you will notice that he began to build them up and to call them into what God said they should become.

Many times as I travel, I might minister to someone about being a mighty man (or woman) of God. I may continue by saying specific, wonder-filled things that God has planned for that person.

Then I'll occasionally get a letter from someone who is quite angry at me saying, "How could you say that? Do you know he or she is the worst individual in town? Do you know what he did to me and what he is doing to the Body even now?"

I simply say to them, "God speaks those things that are not as though they are." (Rom. 4:17.)

God speaks to the potential. What God is building in that person will eventually destroy what is wrong, if they will receive the word and act on it. This is what is called a creative word from God. Creative words, if heeded, will work repentance and lead to deliverance.

That is part of the role of the prophet: To help people identify who they are in the Body and what they are supposed to be doing. Perhaps that man has been bad news because he was searching, restless and feeling out of place and insecure. Maybe he was searching in all the wrong places for an identity, which he could only have in God.

The other offices, the men and women of valor, the Gideons who fight the enemy on the front lines — all need a prophet to speak to them. That is why kings and generals in the Old Testament relied on prophets. Their roles were to rule nations and to fight battles. The prophet's role was to give direction from God, to confirm actions and revelation, and to rebuke when a rebuke was necessary.

Functions of the Other Offices

Jesus is the Head of the Church, our Savior, King and High Priest, but He has appointed the five-fold offices to carry out His instructions, as they are directed by the Holy Spirit. That certainly does not mean apostles, prophets, evangelists, pastors and teachers stand between the rest of the believers and God!

The duties of the five-fold offices operate the other way: They represent God to the Church, not the Church to God. Jesus is our Mediator. The five-fold offices are not set in the Church to mediate between believers and God, but to assist believers in conforming to the image of Christ.

The five-fold offices are not trying to "work themselves out of a job," but bring the stability of leadership to the Body as God establishes His Kingdom. Everyone is not born to lead, else who would follow? Therefore, until Jesus returns, there will always be a need for ministerial headship, leadership and guidance in the Body, until we all come to the fullness of Christ.

> **Till we all come to the unity of the faith and of the knowledge of the Son of God, to a perfect man, to the measure of the stature of the fullness of Christ;**
>
> **That we should no longer be children, tossed to and fro and carried about with every wind of doctrine, by the trickery of men, in the cunning craftiness of deceitful plotting,**
>
> **But, speaking the truth in love, may grow up in all things into Him who is the head — Christ.**
>
> **Ephesians 4:13-15**

As long as the Church is on earth, the five-fold offices will still have a job to do. Any Christian who thinks he is so mature he does not need the five-fold ministry, also does not need to attend church or fellowship with other believers. He is heading for shipwreck.

Believers desperately need one another, and we all need the five-fold offices until we come into the maturing of the Body as a whole.

The prophet gives direction, the apostle oversees and the evangelist adds numbers to the Kingdom by calling the lost to repentance.

The evangelist has been called by God to have a special burden for the lost. Generally, evangelists have had a dramatic experience concerning the reality of hell. They *know* the unsaved are going to hell. It is not a "doctrine" to them, but a literal reality. Sometimes they have had a dream, sometimes a vision, and other times a supernatural exposure to the reality of hell.

Evangelists are sent to the world, first of all. When they hold meetings in our churches, we call those meetings "revivals," which is wrong. To be revived, someone has to have first been born again. Evangelists holding "revivals" minister to the unsaved who are brought in by friends or relatives or have been sitting in the church "incognito," with most of the others thinking they were already saved.

The second thing the evangelist is called to do is teach the Body in general how to win the lost to Christ. If they are not doing that, they are not fully evangelizing. And many evangelists are not aware of that part of the assignment of their office.

Most people think the evangelist is called only to the world, but he is *set* in the Body, Paul said. That means he has a role to play in the Body. He is as much called to the Church as to the world, only in the capacity of teaching how to win the lost. He must train the troops in an area that is not covered by the teacher.

It brings sorrow to my heart to see that far too many evangelists miss the fact that they have this call. For if believers knew they were responsible for evangelizing those around them, the Church would be a different place.

The closer you get to God, the more vulnerable and transparent you become to people. If you are willing to be vulnerable and transparent, you will touch many through your openness and sincerity. The best evangelism is both speaking and living the blessed life of which you speak.

How much would the Church affect the world if Christians were taught how to win others and did not rely on their pastors or ministers to do it all?

A pastor is not to be an evangelist, although he can lead people to Christ. Basically, a pastor is called to be a protector, a father, a teacher, a stationary gift, a guardian and a nurturer of those who already are saved. He is one whose heart is for the Master's sheep.

The prophet, on the other hand, sees what is wrong and what should be done and wants believers, including the pastor, to immediately comprehend and "get on with the program."

The pastor's reply to the prophet's somewhat impatient plea may be that we must realize the vulnerabilities of the sheep. Their needs must be met to allow them the liberty to hear and obey. If a man is hungry, he should not starve to death while listening to you tell him of the excellence of God. First feed him, that he might hear. This is a natural metaphor of a pastor's thought. Lead the sheep to grass and water, and they'll happily graze in your field. Sheer them when necessary to preserve their lives, and they'll love you.

A true pastor is very protective of those believers placed in his care. He does not allow ravening wolves to come in and destroy.

A true pastor also will not allow false prophets or false ministries to occupy his pulpit. But, if he earnestly misses discerning a wolf, the prophet will identify the true from the false.

The teacher, on the other hand, is a knowledge-giver, a strengthener of the Body, one who brings insight into the Word of God. Teachers are concerned with developing the nature of Jesus in believers. They tend to be reason-minded rather than abstract-minded. They have a firm grasp of the basics and great patience. A true teacher does not mind teaching the same thing for years if need be. The teacher's office is more practical, "down to earth," and involved in the mechanics of everyday life than the others.

All of the offices, except for that of pastor, generally are itinerant (traveling) ministries. However, some teachers are stationary, because of their life circumstances, and some pastors move from one church to another for the same reason. Pastors who are eventually called to the apostolic, will find themselves feeling compelled to move out and help establish order in other churches.

When are we going to see the five-fold offices operating in unity, fulfilling Jesus' purpose for them?

When will we hear the voice of the prophet and apostle on television today as frequently as the evangelist, teacher and pastor?

We will see and hear this when we illuminate the misconceptions concerning these offices. When the Church comes into the unity of the believers and believers into maturity in the Word, we will fully begin to take the Gospel to the ends of the earth.

4
The Making of a Prophet

As was previously discussed, prophets must be men and women of an excellent character. Of course, God will use whoever is available to Him, but He manifests a greater anointing through those of good character. There is far too much shallow ministry today, attributable to the fact that far too many in ministry have a shallow relationship with God.

Contrary to what is popularly preached in some circles, God is not raising up people like wild flowers that bloom overnight. "Wild flowers" in ministry often result in "wildfire," or as it is called in the Bible, "strange fire" (offerings to God). (Lev. 10:1.)

It does not take time for you to minister out of the deposit that is presently in you. That only requires willingness and obedience. However, it does take time for maturation and seasoning, which only come as a result of a well-developed relationship with God, revealing a deep flow of His Spirit. If you are born again today, you will not walk in the office of a prophet in two years, though you may definitely exhibit every classic trait of a prophet. Instead, in two years you will just begin the course of development that comprises an accurate, stable, tried and tested, proven minister of the prophetic.

When I was two years old in the Lord, I was fairly accurate in giving prophecies, but certainly not infallible nor accurate enough to occupy the office. I was learning, exercising and growing. I had a fine pastor, but no prophet to teach or help me. Therefore, the Lord Himself had to do it.

Begin where you are and allow God to build you from that point. It did not bother me to wait for years to be used, because it was in God's hands and not mine. It is God Who qualifies you when He deems you ready. The truth is, my greatest problem then was the other extreme from rushing into ministry. I was reluctant to venture forth out of uncertainty and a fear of displeasing God. As I developed fortitude and a greater resistance to fear, God strengthened and greatly increased me. It was several years and numerous errors later that I finally was recognized for the office gift.

Prophets are flesh and blood, a "joint" supplying their part to the Body of Christ. They must be moved by the Holy Spirit, exclusively. A true prophet does not need to wait for a "special" anointing to prophesy any more than a pastor needs to wait for a special anointing to pastor. It is "natural" for a prophet, yielded to the Holy Spirit, to accurately prophesy.

However, prophets must have a keen sense of timing as to the will of God for the moment. It is possible for a prophet literally to prophesy or execute any element of his office at any time, but it is not always permitted by God. I can literally minister prophetically to anyone at any time because I have that spiritual sight. I am just not permitted to, for this gift does not operate at my will but at God's! To do so at will can open the prophet to a perversion of his gift, or cause trouble by giving a word out of season.

Integritous prophets allow God to *make* them that way. It does not come easy or overnight. Though the scripture promises God's yoke is easy, His burden is light (Matt. 11:30), He does not promise the way is easy. God does not *cause* adversity for adversity's sake, nor does He tempt or try you with evil. But He will use the adversity to build you.

Prophets must be steadfast, immovable and unshakable, unaffected when people look at them judgmentally. Maturity dictates that there is no time for self-pity if your words are rejected.

Jesus' words were not only rejected, but *He* Himself was rejected by those closest to Him as well as scoffing skeptics of every generation. They tried to stone Him, and later, His crucifixion was instigated by His own countrymen. Yet He never blamed them nor sought retribution or even exoneration from men. He is the perfect role model for all Christians, and particularly for those of the five-fold ministry.

Prophets must not allow adulation or criticism to move them. Everything that could possibly be said that is good, bad, or indifferent, will be spoken of you if you endeavor to follow Christ closely.

Learn not to be moved by what people say or think. When they're not talking about you is time enough to worry, for that may mean you are doing nothing to upset the devil. A godly, righteous nature will cause conviction to stir your unseen enemy against you. Therefore, learn to rejoice in times of affliction, knowing that the trying of your faith works patience. (James 1:3.) It is becoming increasingly more popular and profitable in this generation to be called a prophet, but when the tests come, only the called will be able to stand.

Prophets must be powerful in this generation, considering the fact that the forces of the enemy seem so overwhelming to the weak. It is puzzling to me how people without Jesus and the Holy Spirit make it in today's wicked world. If ever a generation needed the ministry of the prophet, it's this one.

An excellent example of the making of a prophet can be seen in the life of Elijah, an Old Testament figure whom everyone would agree was a real prophet. He operated in power and was full of faith. He was fearless when facing God's enemies, the priests of Baal, and trustworthy.

However, after Elijah had shown himself so fearless against the false priests, he allowed himself to be shaken by the wrath of Queen Jezebel. It is evident by what transpired when he fled Israel that God was still working on his character. We should be thankful to God that He is not harsh when building our character. His kind nature is proven by His benevolence in sending an angel to minister to Elijah with food and water. (1 Kings 19:5-8.) Don't be fooled. Every prophet will go through his Cherith brook, Jezebel, earthquake, wind and fire experience before he is approved by God! In the midst of his, Elijah defended himself, just as many of us do when the problem is actually a lack of faith, obedience, or self-pity.

The Scripture says:

> **So he said, "I have been very zealous for the Lord God of hosts; for the children of Israel have forsaken Your covenant, torn down Your altars, and killed Your prophets with the sword. I alone am left; and they seek to take my life."**
>
> **Then He said, "Go out, and stand on the mountain before the Lord." And behold, the Lord passed by, and a great and strong wind tore into the mountains and broke the rocks in pieces before the Lord, but the Lord was not in the wind; and after the wind an earthquake, but the Lord was not in the earthquake;**
>
> **And after the earthquake a fire, but the Lord was not in the fire; and after the fire a still small voice.**

> **So it was, when Elijah heard it, that he wrapped his face in his mantle and went out and stood in the entrance of the cave. Suddenly a voice came to him, and said, "What are you doing here, Elijah?"**
>
> **1 Kings 19:10-13**

Elijah repeated his defense from verse 10: "Lord, I have worked very hard for You, and the Israelites have thrown down Your altars and killed Your prophets. I am the only one You have left." (Our prophet had a short spell of amnesia at this point, for the prophet Obadiah had just informed him he was hiding a hundred and fifty prophets in caves, succoring them with bread and water.)

But God chastised Elijah by dealing with his fears and discouragement. He let Elijah know that, actually, He had seven thousand more Israelites who had not worshipped Baal. Elijah was not the only servant of God left in the land. When Elijah came down from the mountain, he had been through what apparently was the last stage of the "making of the prophet" in his lifetime. After that, he did what God told him to do without complaint, showing an excellence of spirit that was quite remarkable.

Be careful of entering into the "Elijah syndrome," wondering if you are the only one who is obedient and faithful. As a veteran of the syndrome, I can honestly say you will ask questions such as, "What has happened to all the others who began the Christian walk with me?" Or, "Why do well-known Christians fall?" Or, "Why does it seem that some people don't have to keep the same standard in Christ as I do, yet they prosper in their exploits?"

However, if you can hear Him, God will say to you the same thing He said to Elijah: "It is not for you to judge My servants, but to obey My commandments.

Look straight ahead. Remain focused on your divine mandate. Only then will you see that you are not the only one serving Me."

Focusing on God instead of the problems creates an atmosphere for deliverance to come. Prophets either learn that or become casualties.

Elijah had to learn that God was not in the trials, symbolized by the earthquake, wind and fire, but in the still, small voice that brought peace. Why did God use an earthquake, wind and fire? To show Elijah (and us) his trial seemed to be as earth-shaking as a quake, as volatile as hurricane winds coming from an undetermined direction or source and as life-consuming as a violent fire, the fire of opposition. We must allow these things to pass and listen for the still, small voice of God speaking peace to the raging circumstances of life.

A young man named Elisha was chosen by God to succeed Elijah (1 Kings 19:19-21), and in the "making of this prophet," God relegated him to approximately twenty years of servitude to the Prophet Elijah. Prophets *must* become dedicated servants. At the Last Supper with His disciples, Jesus made a point of illustrating the necessity of servanthood in His followers' lives. (John 13:3-16.)

Elisha probably came from an affluent family, as could be determined by his plowing with twelve pair of oxen. Yet he humbled himself to serve the austere man of God. He developed not only in servanthood and faithfulness, but in an intense love for God and a zeal for righteousness, exemplified in his love for and loyalty to Elijah.

A Zeal for Righteousness

Prophets many times see things they would rather not see. Yet a true prophet must learn that being zealous for God does not mean taking His place or "playing God." Again, one must handle things according to God's will and instigation.

It has been heartbreaking for me on many occasions to look into someone's face and know it is his last chance to hear the word of the Lord and obey it, or he will die. It is just as grievous to my spirit to give an altar call and get no response from one whose days on earth I know are numbered. That sends me home heavily grieved.

It also is difficult, not exclusively for prophets, but for most ministers, to see the wretched atrocities that are happening in our nation and others. I was unable to watch the Rwandan crisis on television, because I would be moved to uncontrollable tears on behalf of a nation that had turned away from God.

I know now that God is moving there. Nonetheless, they have paid an awesome price for not keeping Him the center of the nation. If people in a country are calling on the name of Jesus, trusting and believing on Him, and establishing God's Word, God will not forsake them. But when heads of a nation make declarations, such as some of our national officials have been making recently, Lord, have mercy upon that nation. God will judge it because of the righteous.

It does not matter who is elected president, if that man does not recognize Jesus as Lord, the country is in trouble. The biblical pattern is to respect leadership, as long as leadership is God-ordained. The Bible also tells us to pray for those in authority (1 Tim. 2:1,2), but it does not say that we must support wrong concepts or actions. If ever there was a need to pray and stand for right principles, it is now!

I believe we are going to see the Church come to a point where we will be *pressed* through common suffering into praying and seeking God in order to change the status quo.

Prophets must use their zeal for righteousness with a full understanding of the love of God and how He is implementing that move through the Holy Spirit. We will see that, just as with the Prophet Samuel, prophets will both orchestrate and teach the "how to" of flowing in the Holy Spirit.

Elisha went through an intense period of training as God constructed a prophet contemporary to his time. And let's be perfectly honest, Elijah probably was not the easiest person in the world to serve. We are not told much about his personality, but we can assess that he was very forceful, odd, demanding and commanding. As all true visionaries, he desired his servant to hand him the baby without the labor pains! All of the kings in the vicinity were terrified or highly respectful of him during his lifetime. I am sure that Ahab, king of Israel, was very glad when the chariot of fire came from Heaven and took Elijah.

Despite the fact that the Church has not reached her full potential in America today, when my husband was national press secretary for the Pat Robertson campaign for President in 1987 and 1988, we discovered the national media was afraid of Christians and still is. They do not know how many of us there are, nor do they comprehend our strength. (That should come as no surprise to the persevering saint, for we, the Church, have no idea how powerful and viable a force we really are.)

However, the press set a snare. They determined to stop Pat Robertson by exploding the news about Jimmy Swaggart, which most of them had known about one full year earlier. They timed the breaking of that y to stop Robertson, because of his radical stand for

Christianity. In a sense, Pat Robertson became a prophetic voice, calling the system back to its ancient roots in God. And just like Elijah, the Jezebel system determined to put him out of commission. However, the oppressor only caused Pat to be disbursed abroad, establishing organizations and programs that are dramatically impacting this government and the world. God raised up seven thousand with Elijah and millions with Pat!

The Church does not have any idea of the "muscle" she has. We must begin to exercise our abilities in God. We must draw together in a corporate anointing, unified for purpose. The Church desires to exercise power, but the price of power is unity. If we desire to see governments hear the words of the prophets as in Elijah's day, we must unify as one common Christian voice, despite our doctrines. Our base for unity begins with our agreeing that Jesus Christ is Lord. This will cause to return the days of miracles.

A prophet who has been nurtured by God over a period of time will manifest an intense love for God and for His people. I have met some who called themselves prophets, but who had no love of God in their hearts at all. They commit adultery, fornication and all manner of transgression without fear. Someone with a true love for God will love righteousness, hating even the garment spotted with sin. (Jude 23b.)

Once I ministered to a young man who was heavily involved in fornication. Yet he could skillfully prophesy the word of the Lord, and was accurate a great deal of the time. That is frightening to me for his sake. God is honoring his ministerial calling, but he will be judged according to how he lives.

That means he will pay the penalty while he is still on earth for his dishonoring of the anointing — if he does not repent and turn from this wickedness. Samson functioned as a judge in ancient Israel, yet enjoyed a lifestyle of fornication and carnality.

God honored his office as long as possible, but eventually, his lifestyle of sin led to his downfall and degradation, all for a moment's passion. His life became forfeited then, and his days on earth were shortened. (Judg. 13-16.)

A Commitment to Holiness

All prophets must be committed to holiness, and this commitment is a by-product of a growing intimacy with God. It is fatal to the ministry to allow transgression and will render powerless the anointing, even though the gift remains operational. True prophets decry sin. They speak about it so often it becomes like a "broken record." Prophets want the people of God to be righteous. They, above all, realize the righteousness and holiness of God. How can mankind hope to relate to God if not by His standards?

However, real prophets understand the enormous stumbling blocks thrown in the way of humanity, attempting to show people how to overcome obstacles put in their paths by the world, the flesh and the devil. Seeing unrighteousness in others and judging those people is "self-righteousness." Seeing unrighteousness and being grieved but compassionate toward the people is true righteousness, keeping as a forethought, "But for the grace of God go I." (Rom. 5:15.)

I was in a large church once in a certain city when the Lord gave me this word:

"There's a certain gentleman in this church who is involved in homosexuality, and this is his last chance to repent. Otherwise, he will die in a few years."

I continued, "I don't need to point you out, but at the conclusion of the message, you need to find your way to the altar and cry out to God for the cleansing of your body and mind. You must start your walk with Jesus, or else your life will be forfeited, your sin will kill you."

I continued the message but was interrupted a few minutes later by a young man sobbing hysterically behind me in the choir. He threw himself upon the altar, saying, "It's me." He was the pastor's son.

Those are the kinds of things encountered while the prophet is in the making. If I had backed away from delivering the warning, the man probably would have been dead by now. Thank God, he did repent and was cleansed. We must be patient with those caught in the snare of certain vices, especially homosexuality. They certainly can be delivered, but it may take years to become totally free from the thoughts and patterns. The same can be true of alcoholism, substance abuse, or other addictions.

Jesus saw the sins of His people more clearly than we see them today, and He pronounced judgment on the nation just before the end of His earthly ministry. Yet, He was moved with compassion even as He prophesied what would happen to them. He wept and travailed over them in their sins out of the intense love that compelled Him to die. (Luke 19:41-44.)

The making of a prophet includes becoming more and more aware of Jesus as He really is. Anyone who preaches for an hour and does not mention Jesus, in my estimation, is not fit to be listened to! John says to try the spirits by the Spirit. If there is no confession of Christ Jesus coming in the flesh, there is no message from God, no matter how profound. (1 John 4:1.)

Prophets in training, or those being made into true prophets (I lovingly call them PITS), learn when to speak and when not to speak. However, they also must be able to give a rebuke when God wills it, just as Elijah and Elisha did. They must have confidence that God will back up what He tells them to do and will empower the office in which they stand. It is an accomplishment to grow in grace to such a place that God would entrust you with this authority.

After Elijah went up into Heaven in a whirlwind, Elisha took off his old cloak and tore it into two pieces. He then picked up Elijah's mantle and put it on. First, this act symbolized his laying aside the old life as servant and apprentice and moving into the full office of prophet. (2 Kings 2:12,13.) Second, it symbolized the taking on of the very covering or identity of Elijah, a thing impossible to do without God's consent.

Soon he came to the Jordan River, which is very deep and swift in places, and with full confidence took the mantle in hand and said, **Where is the Lord God of Elijah?** After this, he smote the waters, and they parted for him the same as Elijah. Elisha walked back over to the other side on dry ground. He proved the mantle. (2 Kings 2:14.)

By this, the "sons of the prophets" who had been watching all this from afar knew that the anointing of the office of Elijah now rested on Elisha. (2 Kings 2:15.) After that, Elisha actually did greater exploits than those recorded of Elijah.

As a prophet develops, he gains a peculiar insight into human nature. When this is wrapped in a love for people, it brings compassion, not judgment. But he needs to be willing to rebuke or to warn at the behest of the Holy Spirit. He also must learn temperance so as not to develop the opposite problem — constantly correcting and rebuking or lacking compassion.

Untempered prophets have what I call a "rain down fire from heaven" mentality. I believe every prophet at one time or another has experienced this extraordinary temptation out of provocation or anger. The judicious side of the prophet desires instant justice or gratification, while the compassionate side seeks mercy. Two excellent scriptural examples of merciless justice are 2 Kings 2:23,24 and Luke 9:54. In both instances, Elisha and Peter felt an injustice was being done to God, or God's authority was being blasphemed. In one instance, Jesus quickly settled the issue with mercy, giving an excellent example of the balance. Elisha's tormentors were not so fortunate, and their youthful tauntings caused a terrible retribution, which, for Elisha, was legal but not expedient.

The prophet must carefully weigh his words against potential outcome. There is a scripture which says you should not be afraid of a prophet who speaks a thing presumptuously and it comes not to pass. That leads me to believe, on the other hand, that a prophet can speak presumptuously and have the thing spoken come to pass! This ability is also available to faith-filled believers, whether prophets or not. (Mark 11:23,24.) God is admonishing us to weigh our words before speaking to get a godly outcome.

I remember receiving a mild rebuke from the Lord for the many times that I have spoken things to people in a pseudo-joking manner, and they have happened. An example: My youngest brother's first child was due on a certain date, days removed from my birthday. I began weeks earlier to confess in a partly playful manner that the baby would wait until my birthday to be born. The anxious mother waited a few days beyond, and to her surprise, the baby was born on my birthday. Now to most of us, we would surmise this event to be purely coincidental. And, I admit, I would also, were it not for the fact that this pattern of presumptuous prophecies coming to pass has happened too many times to count.

Did I cause little Ariel's birth on my birthday? I think not. However, I missed an opportunity to comfort a first-time mother with the knowledge of the day of the birth she anxiously awaited. God's rebuke caused me to approach my jesting more soberly, and the gift is now used in an even more productive manner.

A Prophet Goes Through an Apprenticeship

Ideally, the making of a prophet should involve an apprenticeship of some sort to one who already has been taken by God through the process of maturation. Although Elisha was apprenticed by Elijah, Elijah's mentor is not identified. In some cases, it is not another person but the Lord Himself Who acts as trainer, if there is no human being available to mentor the younger prophet.

The Apostle Paul was trained by Jesus supernaturally, having very little input from the other disciples, nor even by Jesus when He was on earth. (1 Cor. 9:1,2; Gal. 1:1.) However, we must observe that Paul was extensively trained by Gamaliel, a teacher of the law, and extraordinarily educated as a Roman citizen. God simply took all of that foreknowledge and reached Paul where he was, turning him to become the most prolific among the disciples.

The apprenticeship is not just arranged by God to teach the "dos" and "don'ts" of the prophet's office. It is designed to train a prophet in how to submit to authority. If he cannot submit to the natural authorities, he will not submit perfectly to God.

Submitting to natural authorities is not necessarily the most pleasant task, because most of us desire to do what seems right in our own eyes. We seldom want to be told what to do. Yet if we are Christians throughout eternity, someone will be telling us what to do! God's Kingdom is a place of perfect authority and order, not a place of chaos where each person does what seems right to him or to her.

Perfect freedom is only found in total obedience to God.

Elisha submitted to Elijah during his lifetime, and moved out in even greater ways after Elijah was taken to Heaven. While his master was alive, however, you never heard of Elisha doing anything except serving Elijah, and nothing implies that that was an easy task. Elijah's behavior would be considered peculiar by anyone's standards.

He was very dramatic in carrying out his role as a prophet. He bent over laughing at the hundreds of priests of Baal when they were imploring their "gods" to set the sacrifice on fire. (1 Kings 18:27.)

He made fun of them, saying, "Perhaps your god is asleep, or chasing women, or in the bathroom." (Several Bible scholars believe being "occupied" in this context implies being in the bathroom. However, it has not been proven to say so.)

Elijah was one man against hundreds, including the power of the throne. But he got their attention, partially because of his wild appearance and demeanor.

Just imagine Elisha plowing, minding his own business, when a wild man enters the field and throws a garment at his feet, without so much as an introduction. Elijah simply did away with all the amenities. He threw his coat at Elisha's feet and stared at him.

Elisha understood, and he said, "Wait a minute. Let me go kiss my father and mother goodbye," to which Elijah implied, "What has that to do with me?" Then, he turned his back and walked off. Put yourself in Elisha's place, and you too will concur, these few actions herein described accent a colorful, dramatic and somewhat abnormal personality.

He could not have been the easiest person to follow or to live with. Elisha is a perfect example of a good apprentice. That is why he could say that he wanted a double portion of the Prophet Elijah's spirit when Elijah left this earth — and he got it. Only those who are of like revelation and nature can receive the spirit of another. Perhaps it is this factor that enabled Elisha to revere, love and follow Elijah.

Becoming a prophet is not a pleasant, easy process, but the rewards of serving God to the best of your ability and fulfilling your calling make it worth all of the hardships and tests. The only way you can see the fullness of God as Elijah did is to maintain an enormously close relationship with God. To get to that place, you will have to go through many things. It is not just laid at your feet.

Without his total dedication to serving Elijah as Elijah served God, Elisha could not have inherited Elijah's mantle. That mantle symbolized the prophetic anointing and call to speak God's Word with the same accuracy and boldness as Elijah.

Both of those prophets, our classic examples, gave everything to God. Neither of them had wives or children. Both of them suffered adversity and persecution.

How many prophets today have, or would be willing, to give up everything to serve God? It is important to remember when pondering all aspects of the ministry that *God is really in charge.* And just because someone is anointed by God does not mean he cannot make mistakes, and sometimes detrimental ones. It is most essential to understand that the minister must always strive to remain within the confines of his true anointing.

In early 1994, I made a ministry trip to Asia. There my colleague and I ministered to an intercessor, a man who genuinely is a "prayer warrior." Periodically, he would spend hours in prayer for people around the world, as well as for nations, churches and pastors.

However, somehow this wonderful intercessor felt "inspired" to come against the spirit of mammon that is over his nation. In order to divest this money-lusting principality of its power, our friend moved out of his spiritual jurisdiction, and that force nearly destroyed him. He came for assistance, because he was suffering financially, mentally and physically.

When we discovered what he was doing, we questioned, "Did God tell you to do this?" God had not. He had simply decided it was a good thing to do.

He walked into a domain that was not his and entered into warfare against an ancient spirit that had been operating in that area for thousands of years. Alone, he did not have the power or full spiritual authority necessary to end that spirit's control. That was not within his spiritual jurisdiction.

When he was delivered from the oppression of that spirit, we advised him, "Intercede for the things which God tells you and sensitively be directed by the Holy Spirit. Focus in on your true call, and God will grant you wisdom." To our knowledge, he is doing fine.

A wise prophet and mentor of mine once taught that Stephen may have died a premature martyr's death by stepping out ahead of his calling. Now, before you allow your theological prejudice (as I first did) to dismiss the possibility of any truth to this premise, let's examine his situation. Stephen was called first as a deacon, a servant apprentice. He loved the Lord, was laboring hard in the ministry, but deliberately positioned himself to contend with religious sects. (Acts 7.)

Although Stephen was anointed by the apostles, he was not initially set in the apostolic office. Therefore, he moved out as a deacon to function as an apostle. It is clear to me that Stephen showed all of the classic characteristics of the apostolic call. He was powerful, well versed in the law, a commanding speaker, converted to Christianity and quite zealous. Stephen's gift of special miracles identified his apostolic destiny. There was but one essential missing: A face to face encounter with the Lord.

As eloquent, historically accurate and powerfully presented as his speech was (Acts 7:2-54), it did not contain the name of Jesus nor any provision for repentance to gain salvation. Instead, it was inflammatory and accusative without compassion. Where was the mercy of God that calls men to repentance? Further, even though Stephen was commissioned by the laying on of hands by the apostles, he went out alone instead of two by two. He had an apostle's call, anointing, demonstrative power, but no seasoning!

Many others from Elijah to Paul and Peter received threats of death before their time, but the call, the seasoning and the divine protection for purpose given by

God stayed the hand of premature death. They functioned within the confines of their domain.

Stephen's martyrdom was not in vain, of course, because his heart was right toward God. God will even use our mistakes to His glory when our intent is to do right. A young man named Saul who held the coats of those who stoned Stephen became the Apostle Paul. Samson killed more of the enemy in his death than during his life. However, the best way to live is not to make mistakes of timing and self-will that God has to turn for His benefit or ours. The price of grave error can be deadly.

Because of the Old Testament writings, we can perhaps see the making of prophets more clearly then than in our own time. However, the process and the principles are the same. *If* you are careful to operate where God places you, observing your seasons, remaining steadfast, you will not die until you finish your course.

None of the biblical leaders were killed until they had accomplished all that God intended *except* those who fell into sin (Balaam, Samson and various kings) or those who moved out of their domain, (entering into an area of dominion prematurely).

Paul had many attempts made upon his life, but lived until he could say he had completed his assignment, being careful to stay in the center of God's will, timing and purpose.

From the Heart of a Prophet

It is important to know and to understand that young novice prophets go through many phases of changes before becoming a finished product. Many PITS (prophets in training) were not fortunate enough to have a school based on the prophet's mantle like the one that I have founded and begun.

Prophets go through a period of time where God is establishing the fact that He has called them and is going to mightily use them. In those early days, everything the prophet asks for seemingly is given him by God. Faith begins to soar at an all-time high as God develops the spiritual muscle of the trainee. Just when you feel as though you've got a handle on this thing, God shows that He alone is God and shifts into another gear.

I remember going through a period of time when God would grant me from the simplest answers to the greatest requests, just for the asking. Many miraculous healings took place in the ministry. Furthermore, I could go to a place that never served ice cream, ask for a chocolate sundae, and I would be the only one to receive it!

Of course, I know that you can clearly relate to my juvenile illustrations. You can remember being humbled by the reports that the one who was terminally ill one day received your prayers and faith, and suddenly turned toward a complete recovery. The child who fell and broke an arm received your faith-filled prayers, and the new set of X-rays showed no break whatever!

Then suddenly, something changes, and you are forced to dig deeper and search harder for the presence of God. Your hunger for Him becomes insatiable. But simultaneously the church fathers, who once believed in your extraordinary potential, now have determined that you are a fraud and don't fit anymore. It was fine as long as you were a missionary or even an evangelist, but you, especially you women, cannot possibly be called as a prophetess!

As God begins His breaking and molding process, people become less tolerant of your errors (and they will be many), and more critical of your immaturity. Where does a budding prophet go to learn and grow in an atmosphere that is not hostile toward his juvenile status?

For the Prophet Samuel, it was going to Eli, a man so distant from the current move of God, that a little child, called to the prophetic, had to assume the responsibility of an adult in prophesying Kingdom affairs. (1 Sam. 2:12-17; 1 Sam. 3:1-21.) This entire scenario would scream at any of us that mother Hannah missed God's will, but this could not be further from the truth. Why would a loving God Who had shown so many miracles earlier seem to place you, the budding prophet, in a potentially hostile environment?

The answer has something to do with the law of refinement. Every budding prophet is a diamond in the rough, but every diamond begins as a lump of sooty clay. Being placed in a highly pressurized environment causes extreme heat and extraordinary pressure to press the sooty clay together, forming coal granules in the darkness. And so, when the pastor is critical, or the church mother insulting, just know, PIT, that your "grains" are being pressed together. When husband thinks you are strange, and wife wants a divorce, not desiring a minister for a husband, please feel the grains bonding under pressure.

Many days the budding prophet will find himself prostrate before God, imploring Him for his personal situation. During this time, God begins to develop in you the compassion for others that will cause your intercession to break bondages over nations. Your hunger for God increases, and you come into your own, determined that God is able to do anything.

The Church must grow out of the convenient mentality that says if you go through any suffering, it is because you have no faith. Indeed, that argument would not hold water with any of the patriarchs of the early Church. Don't think for a moment that it was easy for Samuel to be taken from his doting mother's arms (he was, at the time, a first and only child), and be placed in a cold temple with a man whose sons were decadence reinvented! But, all of this made him the prophet of whom God said, "I will not allow one of your words to fall to the ground." (1 Sam. 3:19.)

God will only hide His face from us when He desires us to seek Him even more. Scripture says you will ever surely find Him if you seek with *all* of your heart. (Jer. 29:13.) Yes, it is within God's plan for you to be chased by your Saul; rebuked by your Ahab; loved by your Elisha; betrayed by your Judas; slain like your Savior (dying to the flesh); and raised to your potential by the Father Himself.

Suddenly, you find that, despite no mentor of the kind you desired, God managed to train you, and He used the strangest equipment of all — your life experience. God used the difficult, challenging teacher at school, the Sunday school teacher who wouldn't let you get by, the best friend who led you to salvation, the pastor who felt you were totally off and dismissed you. They were all His tools.

God will begin to place in your life people who think like you, minister like you and are strong like you. You won't feel strange because your highs seem so high, and your lows seem so low. As you persevere and continue to seek, the miraculous begins to happen, and this time on a steady, even keel for you. The diamond is now a finished product ready to be mined.

Transition from one point to another is always painful for prophets. We are creatures who demand change but don't like it. When you were coal in the darkness of your ignorance of God's ways, you became comfortable. But, the miner is now making a demand on your substance, and you can no longer remain in darkness. But, those things you learned in the dark (in secret) now you are released to shout it from the housetops. (Matt. 10:27.)

Now, things are in place, you have become seasoned by experience. And now, Samuel, you are called upon to represent the nation. You are to prophesy to future leaders who aren't even aware of their call. How? You've been where they must go. You've come out of the PIT and have been placed on display, only to be cut and shaped, and finally set in a mounting.

Don't despair for the difficulties, and don't feel that you are losing your mind. But, just know that your suffering, errors, stirring and wrestling will cause you to be fit to command the principalities that rule over nations. Only one willing to pay the price will gain this honor.

At whatever stage of development you find yourself, as you read this book, simply see yourself in its pages, and be grateful you're not alone. God will thoroughly prepare you before He puts you on display.

5

Apostles and Prophets in the Bible

Most people do not realize that there were apostles in the Old Testament as well as in the New. The principles of God demand that everything be done according to the pattern in Heaven. (Heb. 9:1-6,11.) Since this is true, then Solomon's statement from Ecclesiastes is also proven to be true: **...There is nothing new under the sun** (Eccles. 1:9). The New Testament is simply the Old fulfilled.

There is a book called, *The History of the Jewish Religion* (multiple authors, available at Cokesbury Book Stores), that devotes an entire section to the scriptural breakdown of the order of the Shalliach, or pre-New Testament apostles. This book shows the apostolic order of the early priesthood, outlining their duties and requirements.

In the same manner, God used the very same classifying endowments to confirm who in the Old Testament was actually an apostle. These are a few of God's requirements:

1. The apostle must be born with a firm, strong leadership potential.
2. They must be spiritually astute, not fearing man but God.

3. They must have a face to face, life-changing encounter with God.
4. They must know the law.
5. They must display special miracles.
6. They must show judicial and governmental abili ties.

Judging from our list, there is not nearly as much difference between Old and New Testament apostles and prophets as one might assume. The functions of the two offices are much the same in both eras:

• Old Testament prophets pointed toward the cross and had jurisdiction over nations. They had a voice in governments and access to kings. In other words, they were the voice of the Lord to the people, and they prophesied of God's plans and purposes.

• New Testament prophets show Jesus *after* the cross. God did not then stop providing a way for His voice to be heard by His people. Jesus simply fulfilled the prophet's words. Because of the Holy Spirit within us, now God's people can hear Him directly. However, prophets after Jesus' day are still being used to prophesy of, or to interpret, God's plans and purposes.

• Old and New Testament prophets stand in positions of judges, counselors and spiritual as well as natural authorities. There are prophets today, however, who are not aware of this function of their office and thus do not exercise this aspect of their call.

As was stated earlier, the order of *the Shalliach* was pre-New Testament apostles and prophets who were the equivalent of apostles today. Elijah and Moses qualify as our best examples. Both were prophetic and chief leaders who spoke to the heads of state of the nations.

In examining Elijah's qualifications, we see a number of special miracles. On Mount Carmel, Elijah called down fire from heaven, and on other occasions, raised the dead. He established ministries, raising up the sons of the prophets as well as Elisha. So powerful was Elijah's ministry that on the Mount of Transfiguration, he was sent by God along with Moses to counsel Jesus concerning the final events of His earthly life. (Matt. 17:3.) His exit from this life in a blazing chariot totally eluding death shows a remarkable intimacy with God shared by few. Likewise, it shows how close and intimate the fellowship.

Moses also shared intimately with God, which qualifies him as an Old Testament apostle. Moses literally established the order of Israel, raised the priesthood, trained the leadership of the nation and dispensed special miracles throughout his ministry. Moses was the prophet (apostle) with whom God said He personally met face to face. (Ex. 33:11.)

So obviously, an apostle is more than just a messenger who establishes works and ministries. Otherwise, many Christians would be apostles by the establishment of their works, ministries, Christian businesses, etc. Therefore, works alone do not establish one as an apostle.

In addition to establishing works, ministries and churches, an apostle is noted for special miracles and for bringing a profound word to his generation. This was true in the Old and New Testaments and is still true today.

Therefore, we can see that performing great signs and wonders is one of the signs of a true apostle, no matter what dispensation. Everything Jesus taught was justly God's Word in the Old Testament revealed in its fullness. Jesus gave the revelation of what already had been laid as the foundation.

When the disciples began to be called "apostles," the office was not new to them. They understood that order of service to God from the Old Testament. They also understood their function, which was to raise up sons to the call of God and encourage as well as build the leadership, along with all of the other functions previously mentioned.

The Shalliach studied constantly and dispensed knowledge and information to the people. They were among the division of priests who administrated the laws. The prophets whom God raised up later did not just remain in the Temple, but carried this responsibility and this function out among the people. As Israel split into two nations, Israel and Judah, the people no longer came into the tabernacle or Temple except for annual feasts. In God's goodness, He sent representatives out among the people, beginning with Samuel.

Although you will not see the word *Shalliach* in the Old Testament, the concept is intertwined throughout. It would be a deviation from the main focus to pursue the teaching to the fullest. Therefore, I invite you to study the concept as mentioned in the book, *The History of the Jewish Religion*.

The usual definition for an apostle, even among those who believe there are apostles today, is: "A special messenger sent, an establisher of churches and other works." However, the Apostle Paul enhances the definition of an *apostle* this way:

> **Truly the signs of an apostle were accomplished among you with all perseverance, in signs and wonders and mighty deeds.**
>
> **2 Corinthians 12:12**

Times of the Prophetic

We can see that God has always assigned someone to interpret or prophesy His plans and purposes to the people, and to lay foundations for the direction in which He desires to move. However, many of the greatest men and women of God were raised up in times of trouble.

Certainly Moses was called in a time of great trouble. He operated in the function of an apostle/ prophet and his brother, Aaron, was called by God as a prophet for Moses and a priest to the Israelites. (Ex. 7:1.) Then God combined those functions in the office of *judge* for about four hundred years. At the conclusion of this era, we see prophets in the order of Samuel arising, and God sometimes dividing the functions between prophets and kings; i.e., King David.

Elijah's ministry was birthed in tumultuous, troublesome times in Israel. The more prophetic voices God brings forth, the more tumultuous the times. It is also a fact that when God is about to bring about change, a preponderance of prophetic and apostolic voices will arise. Whenever leaders fall, prophets arise.

Elijah operated the school of the prophets, potentially the same ones that Samuel raised in his day. We are not told how many prophets were in Israel in Elisha's time, but we are made aware of the fact that in one small place alone, there was a group of fifty.

We can judge the wickedness of the society around us by the "barometer" of how many ministry gifts God sends into the earth. Paul wrote that where evil abounds, grace much more abounds. (Rom. 5:20.)

In Elijah and Elisha's day — as well as during the times of other Old Testament prophets — people were following other gods, indulging in subverting justice (read the book of Amos), offering their children to Molech, and indulging in all manner of carnal sins.

In the world today, there is not one nation founded on God or committed to following the law of the Lord, much less in the "fear and admonition" of the Lord. Even those nations previously committed to God have deviated from their roots.

People today follow other gods, including "mammon" (lust for things and a love of money). It is easy to see all of the subversion of justice that occurs in the United States and other nations, as well as blatant indulgence in carnality. Wrong has become accepted as "right," and right (the Christian way) is considered "wrong" today by a large cross-section of society.

If we think we are not sacrificing our children to the god Molech, think again! Every time an unborn child is murdered through abortion, it is the equivalent of an offering to Molech. We literally throw them into the fire, through not only abortion, but drug and alcohol abuse during pregnancy, unwanted, abandoned children and illegitimate, unmarried parents. (There is no such thing as an illegitimate child, though there are many illegitimate parents.)

Russia was known as a Christian nation for centuries, but turned to godlessness during World War I. Within fifty years of becoming communist, the Soviet Union became one of the coldest, most desolate and bleakest places on the face of the earth. When a person or a nation turns from God, the Bible says that He **shall hold them in derision** (Ps. 2:4). That means He laughs at this calamity.

However, when people repent and turn from their wicked ways, God moves on their behalf. (2 Chron. 7:14.)

I believe many citizens of the Soviet Union sought God in repentance for their country before communism's control was broken. In the years since the Iron Curtain fell, a number of ministers have spoken a word from God to the Soviet leaders.

Today, I am only aware of one truly Christian president, the Honorable President Fredrick Cheluba of Zambia, South Africa. He has made an open, public declaration to millions that Jesus Christ is Lord over Zambia and that he and his house will remain established in that covenant all the days of his life. Yet, his nation is fretted with troubles and ripe for the greatest move of God in its history. Seeing a historical event such as the election of a true Christian president should solicit from each of us, as Christians, a determination to pray for all heads of nations, and for God to raise up prophetic voices to set the order over the nations.

But, no matter how bad things appear, we can count on one thing: God always will have His overall plan and purpose fulfilled in the earth. The only question is whether we will be part of what He is doing.

The first time the word *prophet* is mentioned in the Bible, it is applied to Abraham. Most people do not think of Abraham as a prophet, yet God told Pharaoh that he was. (Gen. 20:7.) The entire world was full of darkness, and there was no nation established in God at that time and never had been.

Divine Confrontations

All who are called of God to exemplary or extraordinary ministry have come by way of divine visitation or confrontation.

Samuel is an example of how God sometimes calls individuals dramatically. It stands to reason that those who are called dramatically or through a divine confrontation — Abraham, Moses, Samuel, Saul (renamed Paul) — cannot possibly miss knowing God's will for their lives.

Everyone called by God to an office experiences some form of supernatural enlistment. Some are called by a "witness" in the Spirit or by hearing the "still, small voice" of the Holy Spirit. Others are called through a divine, direct confrontation with God.

Abraham was called by God directly, then had several "divine confrontations" with Him — while cutting the blood covenant, a visitation before the destruction of Sodom and Gomorrah, and at the time he offered Isaac up to God. (Gen. 15, 18, 22.)

Moses was confronted by God, Who spoke to him out of a burning bush in the wilderness. (Ex. 3:1-4.) Although Scripture does not say how Moses learned of his heritage, I believe Jochebed, Moses' mother, told him again and again that he was a Hebrew and that God had miraculously spared his life. Therefore, it was concluded, he must have a special task to do for God. Pharaoh's daughter adopted Moses, but his mother took care of him until he was weaned (from three to five years of age).

Samuel heard God speak to him in an audible voice as a young boy living in the tabernacle. He had been given by his mother to be an apprentice to the high priest, Eli. (1 Sam. 3:1-18.) Eli had grown so lax and apathetic in his duties that he allowed his sons to abuse and use the people, even to the point of having sex with women who came to sacrifice at the tabernacle. They also took God's portion of the sacrifices for their own.

It is unfortunate that God had to raise up a child to prophesy to the nation, because the priest was too insensitive to hear His voice. Eli should have been the "iron that sharpens iron," but instead, Samuel had to receive his training directly from God. But all of this fit God's purpose for Samuel's life. It taught him how to depend on God from his early childhood and how to endure in difficult times. He would need it to lead in Israel.

The Apostle Paul in the New Testament had one of the most dramatic encounters with God recorded in the Bible. Many impetuous, anxious, soon-to-be servants of God get the impression that men like these just sprang up full of power and integrity overnight. That is absolutely not true. All of them went through years of intense preparation to be made into the prophet or apostle that God wanted.

Paul's training began when he was slain in the Spirit by a confrontation with Jesus on the Damascus Road. (Acts 9:3.) Then he experienced a miraculous healing of the blindness that had come as a result of that encounter. God placed the scales over his eyes to symbolize that he had been spiritually blind all the days of his life prior to his visitation.

Ananias, a "disciple," laid hands on Paul three days later for his healing. (Acts 3:17.) Then, after first submitting himself to the disciples and spending time in the wilderness alone being taught by Jesus, he moved out into ministry. During the remainder of his life, he experienced much suffering, including beatings, stonings and hunger, as well as shipwreck. (2 Cor. 11:25.)

In addition, Paul was rejected and persecuted by his fellow Jews and constantly battled demonic spirits. In Ephesus, he wrestled with the worshippers of Diana, a "goddess" (demon) called Isis in ancient Chaldean, Babylonian and Egyptian cultures. (Acts 19:24-35.)

By the way, Isis is still around today, and not just in New Age or pantheistic circles. She is included in the Masonic "religion." Every time you see a Masonic Bible, know for a fact that Isis lives. Freemasonry is a wicked secret society, a diabolical earthly religion.

However, Paul was not afraid of what people or demons could do to him. Rather, he feared more the One Who was able to put his body and soul in hell. (Matt. 10:28.) When you come to the point where you no longer fear death, you can do anything for God.

Even before the actual "call," God had begun to guide his chosen vessels through the medium of life experiences. I would estimate that every true prophet, apostle, or minister of stature in God's Kingdom, has had extraordinary life experiences and structured training specifically ordered by God to prepare him for his unique call.

God Uses Life Experiences as Training

As far as we know, Paul was not inducted into God's service nor set apart as a child, as Samson and Samuel were. Yet, like Moses, I believe God was already inducting the boy named Saul into His service. The influences in his early life helped shape him for the role of prophet and apostle, just as the influence of both his natural and adopted mothers did on Moses.

As one walking in the office of a prophet, I distinctly remember hearing God talk to me as a child. I spent many hours by myself, and my parents thought I was "peculiar," a lonely child. I was the middle child of three children, and I strived to achieve success to a much greater degree than the other two.

I was also the one most interested in peace and balance. If things were out of order, or if someone was upset with me, I was miserable. I wanted to be accepted. Through this, God gave me a hunger that could only be satisfied in Him.

I have personally experienced many divine confrontations and visitations, which confirms to me the necessity of them in the lives of the called. One particular visitation comes to mind that totally changed the course of my life.

In the early 80s, John Gimenez of Rock Church, Virginia Beach, Virginia, was inspired of God to call the nation to prayer. It was moving to see hundreds of thousands of people soliciting God's touch to the nation. This was history in the making.

At the conclusion of the rally, everyone was asked to join hands in small groups to sing the closing hymn. At the conclusion of the singing in obedience to our closing speaker, we embraced each other saying, "Jesus loves you and so do I." In our small group of six, three of us had come together, but the three that joined us were strangers. However, one man among the strangers stood out. As we embraced one another in the circle, I could not help but notice that this gentleman prayed for my two companions. When he came to me, he embraced me, pulled away and instead of saying, "Jesus loves you," he spoke, "I love you." My eyes became fixed on his, and in a moment's time, I literally saw my whole life flash before me, reflected in his deep gaze.

At the conclusion of the vision of my life, I saw the word *forgiven* flash in a bright red light over every deeply sinful event, and then everything turned to a brilliant white. He embraced me again, prayed without ever saying a word, and then departed with his two companions. When but a short distance away, he turned and pointed, saying, "I'll see you again, soon." And he did!

I cannot explain how Jesus could manifest in that manner anymore than Paul could explain seeing Him on the Damascus Road or reflected in Stephen's eyes. But I can say that this unusual, divine visitation set the course for all that is supernatural and prophetic for the rest of my life.

Moses received his training backwards according to what we'd assume is the order for most prophets or apostles. First, he had an extraordinarilystructured training in the role of leadership in the palace of Pharaoh. *Then,* he got his apprenticeship in learning to be humble, to be content to just be a servant, if that is what God wanted. All of his training for the first eighty years, however, was through life experiences.

He had to learn to be a yielded shepherd, to have a heart for people, and to know that one person cannot take law and justice into his own hands. He experienced total defeat forty years before he became victorious in his own life. But, the place that he experienced his greatest defeat was the same place he experienced his greatest victory.

From Moses' life, we can see that to be used completely by God, any five-fold ministry gift must undergo "a wilderness experience." Actually, this is true of all believers who are determined to carry out the Great Commission. (Mark 16:15-18.) Jesus especially went through a "wilderness experience."

Moses' forty years was a type of Jesus' forty days in the wilderness. Your wilderness does not have to be a place of no shrubbery, no rain, or beauty. However, it is a place of solitude, a place that causes you to press in to God. That is the purpose of wilderness experiences: to bring us closer to God, not to make us suffer. In our wilderness, God's presence must be sought for diligently. He is seemingly not conveniently available, though ever present.

The very thing that had been Moses' protection, Pharaoh's power and authority, was the thing he came to fear. It took the revelation that his natural protection and natural training and abilities were not enough to bring him victory in life, for Moses to be ready to submit to God at the burning bush.

Everyone called of God is going to have a "burning bush experience," a time when you will meet Him face to face, or you will never know Him to the degree necessary to be "an earth shaker" and a history maker (as Evangelist Tim Storey would say). You must come to the end of yourself before you can be a vessel for God's use.

This process — failure, humility and servanthood, meeting God and becoming submitted and obedient — is what it takes for someone to achieve the higher realms. God is a consuming fire that you either choose to become part of or be consumed by. (Deut. 4:24; Heb. 12:29.)

Jesus aptly put it another way. He said that you either fall upon the Rock or the Rock will fall upon you. (Matt. 21:44.)

In order to be a mouthpiece for God, to function under the prophetic anointing, or just to be a laborer in God's vineyard, you must choose to become part of the fire. You cannot follow from a distance and be great in the Kingdom of God.

Once while studying the life of Samson, the Holy Spirit said to me:

"I called Samson from his mother's womb to be a Nazarite, totally dedicated to Me, and a judge in Israel. However, he chose to follow Me from afar. He actually was cold, but I did not withdraw from him. I needed a judge in Israel, and he was the one I chose.

"He had certain qualities and characteristics which I placed within him, and I gave him every opportunity to get his life in order. But he chose not to do it until the end.

"Therefore, I used him to judge Israel and to judge the Philistines. And I will do the same thing with you."

God's warning here relays to us that His desire is always that we become a part of the flame rather than be consumed by it. Samson was given to God in the womb (his mother consecrated herself as a Nazarite as she carried him) and obeyed the outward vow, but never fully committed inwardly. His vow expressed that he should never, for the duration of his life, break it.

Yet one day, he occasioned an acquaintance who proved to be his undoing. Delilah, whose very name means "lustful," lived in the valley of "Sorek," or choice vine. Samson, carried away by lust, laid his head in the lap of sin's pleasure, losing his hair. And, finding comfort, he allowed Sorek's plumpest fruit to become the meal of his broken covenant vow. In so doing, he fell since God said, "Do not partake of the fruit of the vine." Lustful Delilah was Sorek's (choice vine) most tantalizing fruit.

However, God still used him to judge Israel, and He will use us at our expense if we choose to disobey rather than obey. Samson entered in at the end because God said he was cold. Cold or hot enables Him to deal with you. Lukewarm is vomited out. (Rev. 3:16.)

There is a principle of God established here in Samson's story. God chooses whom He will use, and if you are truly called, He will not exclude using you because of your coldness and inconsistency. Did you ever wonder why certain ministers can live unclean, adulterous lives and still perform miracles, moving under a notable anointing?

There is a principle of God vividly shown in Samson's story. Israel and God needed a leader. God will not disappoint the faithful who believe He will move through the vessel in question just because of that minister's failures. I call it the "Samson syndrome." However, just as with Samson, God will cause you to pay your vow in this life to escape like judgment in the life to come.

Then the Holy Spirit caused me to look at Moses.

Moses literally had the best of everything at his disposal in one of the greatest kingdoms of men on earth. But God enabled him to find his heritage by arranging for his own mother to care for him in his early years.

I imagine as she nursed and cuddled him, or attended to his little wounds, she rehearsed the story of how he was fished out of the river. Destiny drove him to seek out his people. But, when he tried to take destiny into his own hands, his own people turned against him. Fleeing for his life, Moses felt his gravest defeat.

But, only after Moses went through the wilderness could he meet God in the burning bush. God sent him right back to the place where he had experienced his greatest defeat, only to glory in his greatest triumph.

God never removed His hand from Samson or Moses. In the end of his life, Samson drew nearer to God than in the entire duration of his life. In the last third of his life, Moses did the same. We should all behave as Paul, who set his face like a flint toward God, once Jesus apprehended him, or even like Moses. Never take the chance of living like Samson and repenting just before it is too late. That option is not promised, and

God alone knows the number of our days. It is even more dangerous to be like Balaam, to know what is right and end totally wrong. God did everything within His power to stop Balaam except override his right to make his own choices. God will never force you to do what is right.

Paul, like Moses, received his structured training first in becoming a natural leader in his nation. He became a great rabbinical teacher as a student of one of the greatest Jewish rabbis of history, Gamaliel. (Acts 22:3.)

God used Moses' leadership training in his role as the establishing governor of the nation of Israel. He used Paul's enormous education in his role as a foremost teacher and establisher of the covenant of Christ. The works of these two men will live eternally through every generation and beyond Christ's return.

6
Apostles and Prophets in the Age of the Prophetic

Just as prophets are much more than those who see into the future, apostles are more than just "special messengers sent," the typical definition given for the apostle. It is beginning to be apparent that God is saturating the Church with prophets and apostles in preparation for how He is about to move in the 21st century.

This move of God will finally set the prophet and the apostle in their proper positions in the Body of Christ. This has been consistently prophesied for at least the last ten years.

The Church needs all of the five-fold ministry gifts more than ever in its history. In my estimation, this is a chief indication that Jesus is not returning immediately. The great number is a sign that something phenomenal is happening worldwide.

The Holy Spirit spoke to me concerning the eminent return of Jesus, saying, "Why are you anxious for Him to return when two-thirds of the world is not aware that He came the first time?" As I focused on the words, I became heartbroken for the wasted focus of the average believer, me included. I began to focus on the right things — getting the message to the maximum amount of people. It is only then that we will see His return.

Therefore, in preparation, an abundance of five-fold gifts have been released to saturate the earth. As God rightly positions the apostle and the prophet in the Body, we will see a thinning of the saturation as He causes them to be dispersed abroad.

It is necessary to have all five offices in place to accommodate the millions of people who are yet unsaved and untaught. The Church is out of order, because of these missing links. At best, she has been getting little more than half of the messages God desires to send to and through her. That missing half contains the prophetic flow and the laying of foundations which will set the Church in order.

I reiterate, God, in establishing a new move preparatory for Jesus' return, will be calling an even greater number of apostles and prophets than He has ever called. The demand will be greater because the time is shorter. We must set aside fleshly pride and realize that we are the vessels chosen. We are not called for ourselves, but for God's purpose in reaching people and salvaging nations.

As was said earlier, God has focused His attention upon the seed (of mankind) and upon the nations. This has been so graphically demonstrated in the enormous revivals that are taking place, particularly in third world nations. Recently, a prophetess, Dr. Paula Price, and I had the unique pleasure of ministering to the Spirit-filled Christian president of the nation of Zambia, in South Africa. He is a very gracious man, but powerful — perhaps more so than the other heads of nations surrounding him. He is a president, but a "king" by scriptural terminologies, and a man chosen by God to break the bonds of witchcraft from his nation.

When I first received the call to minister to this man from my pastor, Carlton Pearson, I was deeply moved that God would honor me, and that I could touch one so high in stature. However, God dealt immediately with Dr. Price and me about revering fear more than revering Him. I could only think of the fact that I was virtually unknown from a small town. Who was I to be called upon to potentially affect the destiny of a nation? God's reply was to remind me of the fact that I am only a vessel. Vessels don't have a choice as to what kind they will be while they are in the making. They know what they become only after they're made. They also have little or nothing to do with how they will be used. That sufficiently killed my cold feet. There is simply no room for timidity in the front line of a war.

The ministers who will lead and carry on in this next move must be bold, fearless, sanctified and free of respecting people more than God. This next move is not a trying ground for *if* you are called, but a proving ground for the fact that *you are called.*

Many apostles and prophets have been wandering from church to church, seeking a place to fit. Suddenly, they will find their position. What they were looking for was leadership, complete leadership, that identifies the missing pieces of the structure and rightly places them. These two gifts identify lively stones, helping in the construction of the building of God's house. But with only a few of them in place, it is no wonder many people are misplaced.

Again, you must remember that among all of the true whom God has set in office, you are going to find some false. Some will set themselves in position out of pride, greed, or the terribly mistaken idea that the offices of prophet or apostle are prestigious. They have not understood that the higher the office you hold, the more of a servant you are to the people. You also carry the greater responsibility before the Lord.

Others are mistakenly "appointed" by men, as many theologians believe happened after Judas Iscariot betrayed Jesus and killed himself. The disciples, desiring to replace him, drew lots, and the lot fell on a man named Matthias. However, we never hear anything about him again after that point.

They based the fact that someone should be chosen to replace Judas on scripture. (Ps. 69:5; 109:8.) Then, they prayed and asked the Lord to indicate the right person, using a method often used in Old Testament days by which God would show His will. (Lev. 16:8 and others.) However, many Bible scholars and ministers believe the disciples possibly got ahead of God.

Firstly, Peter proposed this, not the Holy Spirit.

Secondly, though they did evoke the Holy Spirit, they left Him no option of choosing the manner of identifying the replacement that was God's choice. Instead, they cast lots, in *faith,* and the lot fell on Matthias. They had forgotten the power of the Holy Spirit that had most recently fallen upon them all. He could have easily prophetically expressed God's desire in a nest of anointed apostles and prophets! Jesus said, "Don't put new wine in old wineskins, or a new patch on an old garment." (Luke 5:36-38.) You don't need lots when the Holy Spirit is present. You will not find Christians casting lots to get God's opinion any time after this in the Bible.

Thirdly, they prayed incorrectly. (Acts 1:24,26.) Instead of asking God, "Who would You desire?" they asked, "Which of these two whom we chose could be an apostle to help by taking Judas' place?" The lot fell on Matthias. God answered, "He can help. He's been helping since John the Baptist lived. It's obvious he is called. I will ordain him as an apostle at your request." But God replaced Judas with His choice.

Why is it so easy for us to do this kind of thing? First, we decide what we esteem is right, then proceed to carry it out, all the while asking God to bless what *we* are doing. Instead, we need to always *start* with Him, not just end with Him. Inquire of Him His will. After all, it may be the right thing, but at the wrong time.

That is what many believe happened. The disciples chose Justus or Matthias and presented them to God, but God had already chosen Saul, soon to become the Apostle Paul. God elevated His choice to the status of the first eleven. And in many ways, this "thirteenth" disciple surpassed all of the others in works.

God's Choice Is Not Always Our Choice

In this prophetic age, the scenario of the disciples choosing Judas' successor is a good one to keep in mind. We must understand that God's choice for any office will not necessarily be our choice. After Paul's life was turned toward Jesus, much time transpired before Christians trusted him. Other apostles, convinced of his authenticity, had to vouch for him.

Suppose today someone from the Internal Revenue Service who was famous for persecuting Christians, closing churches and in general coming against our rights, suddenly walked into your church and wanted to preach. I'm sure that most of us would be skeptical.

We look at people who are abrasive, rude, or perhaps sloppy about their clothing or appearance, and think God would never use them. The truth is that God looks inside and sees potential we would never see without doing the same through His eyes. He sees "a diamond in the rough," a wonderful spirit that has not been cultivated and matured.

People are like apple seeds. We see an insignificant seed, a tiny little thing in our hands, and perhaps think of one apple. God looks at that same seed and sees an orchard — or many orchards.

Please do not be quick to judge those who say they are apostles and prophets. Allow them to be innocent unless proven guilty. On the other hand, do not be quick to accept everyone at his own evaluation. The safest thing is to judge what they say by the Bible. Do your best to remain sensitive to the Holy Spirit in order to have a witness from Him as to whether this person is legitimately His. And rely on the ministry gifts set in the Body to discern the true from the false. True prophets or apostles should be able to recognize those of like calling, representing them to the Body. If there is a need for development, the five-fold officers should collectively be able to identify and assist the fellow officer. But this will not be accomplished if we do not mature.

Let me say again emphatically, the best layman's test for judging a ministry gift is whether or not he comes preaching Christ. If he does not, he is either false, underdeveloped, or backslidden. If he points to himself and draws people to him, not Jesus, something is wrong. If he brings division, something is very wrong — either with the person, the people to whom he is speaking, or both.

Apostles and prophets today are not to come forth with popular preaching. As the Apostle Paul in the early days of the Church, they will come into the churches and set things in order. They must be prepared to be unpopular, and the church must be prepared to be provoked, and yes, even angered!

When things are set in order, peace will be the result. Confusion and chaos cease, and the church will begin to flow and prosper. Of course, there will be those who bring *disorder* under the guise of prophets or apostles. Their result will be division and disaster, not order and peace. But when the real appears, the false becomes very obvious, like comparing rhinestones to diamonds.

Prophets and apostles carry with them a strong anointing for finances. I witnessed an apostle from the Caribbean, Turnell Nelson, take an offering in South Carolina not long ago. The conference needed about seven or eight thousand dollars for expenses.

However, the service had continued late, and many people had already gone home. My husband and I were sitting in the front row and witnessed the paltry offering that was laid at the apostle's feet. Not even thirty people responded to a request for $100 or $50. No large bills or checks came in the general offering, and all of the money lay in two piles easily visible to us.

To our amazement, the apostle took off his shoes and walked on that money. When they counted the offering, it was the amount needed to the dollar. We will see great signs, miracles and wonders wrought by the hands of apostles in the days to come.

Another thing that will become commonplace in the next move of God is the outpouring of the Holy Spirit upon *all* flesh. Peter said in this age, which began at the Day of Pentecost, the words of the Prophet Joel were being fulfilled:

> **And it shall come to pass afterward that I will pour out My Spirit on all flesh; your sons and your daughters shall prophesy, your old men shall dream dreams, your young men shall see visions.**
>
> **Joel 2:28**

I was in a prophets' seminar once, and a little boy about eight or nine years old was attending. He sat in back of me and wiggled and fidgeted all during the lessons. He crawled under the bench and played games, seeming never to look in the workbook during the entire three days of the school.

However, on the morning when people were released to come forward and exercise the prophetic gift, the little boy arose and joined the line. I am sure I was not the only one curious as to what he would say. Perhaps some thought his parents ought to make him sit down and not interfere with the serious work of the Lord.

However, when his turn came, he chose a man out of the group and said to him:

"You are called to the mission field, but you do not have the money to go. God is sending you to a country where the people have never seen anyone white. And you are going to be the first person to tell them about Jesus. At first, they will reject you, but then they will accept you and ask you to become one of them. You are going to witness to them of Jesus, and everyone in the entire village will get saved and filled with the Holy Spirit.

"God will put the money in your hand, because He wants you to go. He wants that village reached for Christ."

And the little boy went back to his seat and his play.

The man to whom he spoke stood crying and said that he was on his way to Africa, to a village of people who had never seen a white person. He said that until an hour before, he did not have the money to go, but someone came and put an envelope in his hand with exactly the amount of money needed to go.

Joel prophesied, "Young men will prophesy." The child was able to flow prophetically because of the overwhelming presence of the Holy Spirit and his yieldedness.

Joel's prophecy of God's Spirit being poured out on all flesh brings up the question as to whether God calls women into the five-fold offices. For the first five years that I functioned as a prophet, I was operating in that flow while at the same time saying that women cannot function in a foundational or governmental position. I had heard Kathryn Kuhlman and others say this, or similar, but I repeated what the others had taught me. Then, the Holy Spirit corrected me and showed me the truth.

Women as Prophets and Apostles

To begin with, we see that Jesus welcomed women into His ministry, although no women were among the twelve disciples. His selection of all men was not meant to be the criteria for the selection of the five-fold offices forever, any more than the selection of Deborah as judge established a matriarchal order in Israel. If we must use the exact criteria of the first twelve apostles, then all apostles today should not only be men, but they should be Jews!

In those days, how could a prophet, who had chosen a group of disciples to travel and minister with Him, include women in that small, intimate group? Due to prejudice and proper etiquette, His reputation would have been ruined immediately and no one would have listened to Him at all. Not choosing women was a matter of "shunning the appearance of evil," as Paul later advised, more than a matter of spiritual protocol. You will notice that none of the other women mentioned in the epistles traveled with the men, unless they were married and went with their husbands, or traveled at a distance in the company of other women.

The same propriety should be observed today. Women in the five-fold office should not travel with single men who are not their husbands or related to them. It appears evil and leaves the ministry open to ridicule and gossip.

The Apostle Paul's writings were often misused as the "proof" that women are not to be used in ministry. However, if his epistles were read in context and in the light of the social questions he was addressing, we would see that he did more than any except Jesus in the New Testament to free women from bondage. (Rom. 16:6-15.) His writings show that women under the New Covenant are restored to the place God originally created them to be — in partnership with men, as Adam and Eve originally were in the Garden.

He wrote to the Galatians:

> **There is neither Jew nor Greek, there is neither slave nor free, there is neither male nor female; for you are all one in Christ Jesus.**
>
> **Galatians 3:28**

Today, we might paraphrase that to read, "There is now, under the New Covenant in Christ, neither black nor white, rich or poor, male or female. We are all one — the same, equal to one another and in unity — in Him."

We will begin to see husbands and wives operating in team ministries, as Priscilla and Aquilla did. Notice that in at least half the places where this couple is mentioned, she is named first.

This is not a book on the roles of husbands and wives, or men and women in the ministry, so I will not discuss Paul's writings in detail. I will only say that they have been much misunderstood, probably because when the committee of men translated our first generally accepted Bible into English, women were considered by society as second-class citizens.

The *King James* translators allowed their doctrines to influence the translation in places. The Greek word, *kephale*, translated *head* in Ephesians 5:18-23, is not the word usually used in Greek for "one in authority over." *Kephale* means "exalted originator and completer," which is the sense in which Paul was comparing Jesus and the Church to husbands and wives.

If as much attention was given to the fact that husbands are to be as self-sacrificing as Jesus was to the Church and that they are to put forth much effort in assisting their wives to be "completed" or "fulfilled" in the Lord's work, we would have greater unity and less division in the Church.

Archon is the Greek word meaning "leader, ruler, or commander," along with several other words used less often. Most readers of Greek works from about 1000 B.C. to about 600 A.D. (covering the times when the entire Bible was either translated into, or written in Greek) would not have read *kephale* and thought "final authority" or "superior rank." *Kephale* in that sense was used infrequently, and incorrectly, in the "street language" or "common" Greek language.[1]

As to women being apostles, a person named *Junia* is mentioned by Paul, along with Andronicus, as being held in high esteem among the apostles. (Rom. 16:7.) The ending *ia* is a "feminine" ending. A man would have been *Julius*, not *Junia* or *Junias*.

Bible scholars who believe women are to be in subjection to men, or who believe women cannot be used by God in positions of authority, explain *Junia* away.

They say that the word is a "typographical" (or scribal) error. In other words, some scribe copied it wrongly in the early years of the Church. However, most of these same scholars will swear that the Bible is inspired and watched over by the Holy Spirit so that this does not happen. If we are to accept that an error this great could happen, how can we know others that affect equally important questions also have not occurred?

This is a very good example of how "doctrines and traditions of men" can not only influence the way you read the Bible, but the way you translate it. In *The Amplified Version, Junias* has been kept, but the verse has been translated to read, **...Andronicus and Junias...They are men held in high esteem among the apostles...** (Rom. 16:7).

Even many of those who have seen that God will use women as evangelists and teachers will balk at the idea of women pastors, prophets and apostles. They do this in spite of the fact that it is very clear God used women both as prophets and in the authoritative offices in the Old Testament. We are told that we have a *better* covenant in the New, not one with less liberty in the Lord. (Heb. 8:6.)

I believe we are going to see, in this generation, some powerful women of God in all of the offices. Women are going to be setting people free all over the world.

The feminist movements are simply grabbing hold of something God is doing to "liberate" women in His Kingdom, and because they are unsaved or nominal Christians, they are usurpers at best! The devil is using their misunderstanding of what God is doing to create chaos and confusion.

By the time the world catches onto something, God usually has gone on to something else!

I believe we are going to see women used in ministry as we never have before. Jesus totally set women free. It is the devil and world society that have kept us in bondage. If you are a woman called to ministry, do not let yourself be hindered by prejudice.

If the devil cannot stop you by telling you that you are "just a woman and cannot minister," he will tell you that you are too old or too young, too fat or too thin, too black or too white, too rich or too poor, too educated or too uneducated. There will be some excuse to try and stop you.

The good news is that God created women just like Himself, as well as men. Men and women collectively are called "sons" by God. In other words, we all are children and equal in Him.

How can we ignore the power of Miriam's ministry? She was a prophetess also called as an elder in Israel. (Ex. 15:20.) Deborah, also a prophetess, judged Israel, holding the position of the supreme authority of the day. Now I might ask, "Was she a figurehead, or a real judge? Did she hold the same authority as the judges who preceded or followed her?" Yes to the second question, no to the first. Deborah held all of the authority of her office and was ordained of God to the position. If you believe that women can lead and not govern, you argue with God's choice, for He qualified Deborah to rule, and if He changed His mind, He would have said so under the new and better covenant.

We cannot ignore Huldah, a prophetess, who was as crafty and cunning as the "weasel" she was named for. (2 Kings 22:14; 2 Chron. 34:22.)

Anna, the prophetess, heralded the arrival of the Messiah, preaching He had come to her generation. (Luke 2:36.) Philip had four daughters, all of whom prophesied. (Acts 21:8,9.)

John's elect lady was not a mother with a Bible study of her natural children, but clearly a female pastor, or perhaps even apostle. The use of the language directed to her from the apostle John was as an equal speaking to an equal, or a father looking out for one of his children in the Lord. And of course, the book of Acts is pregnant with women in every capacity of ministry.

It is important to understand that in the questionable passages of scripture concerning women's silence in the church (1 Cor. 14:34), usurping authority (1 Tim. 2:12), and even covering (1 Cor. 11:10-15), the translations should rightly read "wife" instead of "woman." Half of the Church world would have come out of the dark ages into the light had they but observed that very obvious little point. These scriptures address wives as opposed to women in general, or address order in the Church and not the demeaning of women.

A very funny thing was spoken over a friend of mine. A certain pastor was one of those who could not accept women in the pulpit. However, a woman prophetess came through his church who had such a profound gift that he could not ignore it. He allowed her to "say a few words" before his message.

She prophesied the word of the Lord so strongly that he was taken aback and went to minister to her.

He said, among other things, "Thus saith the Lord, your expression is great. Your prophetic ability is profound. It is like that of a man!"

Did he hear from God? Yes, he did, but he filtered what he heard through his doctrine that women could not be in that ministry, so the Lord's word came out, "Thou art like a man."

I would caution women in the ministry very strongly, however, to maintain the proper priorities. When I was married with only one child, the Holy Spirit spoke to me one day and said, "Never sacrifice your children on the altar of ministry."

That told me three things:

1. I was going to have more than one child.
2. I needed to watch my priorities.
3. I was going to be ministering throughout my life.

That is a lesson I have never forgotten. I have met women who really are called to ministry and who have mighty ministries, winning souls to Christ all over the world. Yet they have neglected their husbands to the extent that some of their husbands have walked out on them.

Also, I met one woman who would not have physical relations with her husband because she considered him "unholy." He was a Christian, but he had different views of some things concerning Scripture than she did, and he did not think she should be a minister.

I believe the Holy Spirit is saying, "This kind of thing has to stop."

A woman out of order is one of the most destructive forces on the face of the earth. A married woman's first ministry is to her husband; secondly, to her children; and only then to the ministry to which she is called. Men in ministry should realize that the same thing is true of them. When we were all called, didn't God know what our responsibilities as far as family would be? He has already made the provision to see to it that every minister stays in perfect balance.

Observe your seasons, and you will not miss the timing or the purpose of God. The multitudes will be saved, and your family will be among them. There is plenty of time to do it all, and well if you walk in strict obedience to His timing and commands.

Endnote

[1] Trombley, Charles. *Who Said Women Can't Teach?* South Plainfield, NJ: Bridge Publishing, Inc., 1985, pp. 125-133.

7

Prophetic Modes of Delivery

A *mode* is a manner, way, or a method of doing something. In prophecy, there are diversified modes of delivery. Prophecy can be delivered both with and without words, each method being extremely effective. The wordless prophecies include acting out or dramatization, dance and music without lyrics. (It is most effective to hear the instruments prophetically glorify God.) I believe we are going to see more of this style of expression, just as all of the other definitive modes of delivery used by God through His prophets in the Bible.

There are almost as many modes of delivering prophecy as there are prophets, adding a variety of flavors to the prophetic. This is orchestrated by God expressly to keep the delivery of His Word fresh and intriguing enough to keep the interest of the Body. Some of the different "styles" found in scripture are Word oriented and some are physically oriented.

Here are a few examples of what I classify as speech-oriented styles:

• Prose prophecy, such as is found in Isaiah, Jeremiah and Ezekiel.

• Song, psalm, or poetic prophecy, such as in the Psalms, Song of Solomon, Ecclesiastes and Exodus 15.

The physically oriented modes include:

• Dramatized, or acted out prophecy, such as were performed by Jeremiah and Ezekiel. Once the Lord commanded Jeremiah to buy a linen girdle, a band that wound around his waist, and bury it by a river. Later, Jeremiah had to dig it up, decayed and ruined, as an object lesson for what God's judgment would be upon Israel. (Jer. 13:1-11.)

Ezekiel was required to lie upon his side facing Jerusalem more than three hundred and ninety days, symbolizing the years of the iniquity of Israel. Afterward, he was required to lie upon his other side to symbolize forty years of iniquity for Judah. (Ezek. 4:1-9.) He also ate a special grain mixture cooked over cow manure, and drank water, acting out the prophecy that foretold of the Israelites eating defiled bread among the heathen while in bondage in Babylon. (Ezek. 4:10-17.)

There is also the expression of prophecy in dance, as was superbly demonstrated by the prophetess Miriam and company at the drowning of Pharaoh's army. (Ex. 15:12.) And there is the playing of instruments, as demonstrated by Elisha the prophet in 2 Kings 3:14-20.

Prophecy may be written out, long or short, or may be delivered as a prophetic teaching or sermon. Or, prophecy may be sung, as demonstrated through many of the Psalms. A true "psalmist" is a musical, singing, or poetic prophet, not merely a singer or musician. I have observed all of these styles, including poetic prophecy delivered in "rap," a form of today's street language.

Prophets sometimes change tones for emphasis. One may bring a word that sounds an alarm, which may be delivered in a very loud voice, while another's voice may be soft and tender. Volume does not equate or validate the prophecy.

I have seen prophecy dramatized and even had the Lord use me in that manner, as with a pastor in a southern town whom I struck in the chest three times. In that same general area, I delivered another personal prophecy to an astute, though troubled, young man. During special ministry, the Holy Spirit had me call a huge, handsome man out of the audience, and when he had come to the altar, I was directed to, "Grasp him by his tie and throw him!"

I actually grasped him by his tie, and I threw him back and forth before the altar. Of course, there is no way I physically would have been able to do it if I were not under the anointing of God. At the time, I was only a tiny size four.

The word of the Lord to him was this:

"Thus saith the Lord, just as *she* threw you from one place to another, so did I rescue you and preserve your life from destruction and danger. For I am going to rebuild all of your broken walls, and I am going to set in order those things which are out of place, causing to come to naught the wicked plans of the enemy.

"Then, I shall turn your life around, and you will be a blessing to many people, for the gifts within you are going to begin to come forth in a mighty and dramatic way."

The man fell to his knees and cried like a baby. Later, I learned his story. He was a single man who had fallen into a trap set by a woman in a church where he was an organist. She and a family member had decided that the organist should marry the young woman, and they began to practice witchcraft against him.

They invited him to dinner, put something in his food, causing him to become extremely ill, and would not allow him to leave their home. For one solid week, they kept him behind closed doors. After three or four days, he realized something else was wrong in addition to his being sick.

They kept telling him that he had the flu, and that they would call a doctor — but never did. Very soon, he caught on to the fact that, after eating, he became sicker. So he stopped eating and began to regain his strength.

In his weakened state, he attempted to get up and leave. Yet the daughter, a small woman, grabbed him and threw him around the room just as I had under the anointing of the Holy Spirit. However, her power was demonic.

The prophetic dramatization demonstrated to the man that God not only saw what had happened to him but was going to deliver him. He had surmised something was wrong with him, and that he had done something terrible to deserve the kind of treatment he had received at the hand of his captors. He was purged of negative emotions concerning the incident that night in church, and his life was set in order.

In Acts 21:11, a prophet named Agabus acted out what would happen to Paul if he persisted in going to Jerusalem. The prophet took a girdle (a waistband) and bound his own hands with it. This dramatization gave a chilling precognitive actualization of Paul's final arrest, which eventually led to his martyrdom.

Dramatized Prophecy Is Unforgettable

As the man who was thrown by his tie, someone who has experienced a prophecy dramatized for them certainly is not likely to overlook or forget that particular word from the Lord! High technological advancements offer so many entertainment advantages that anything less than dramatic will not totally reach this "now" generation. I'm sure we will see more of this displayed in days to come. We will also see once again prophets speaking concerning the elements, as Elijah pronounced no rain upon Israel (1 Kings 17:1), and it did not rain. We will see prophets pronounce who will or will not be elected to office, and it will come to pass according to their words. I personally have known every president who would be elected, prior to each election, over the years of my salvation.

There is going to be a dramatic manifestation of the will of God as it pertains to nations, because I believe God has focused His attention upon two things: the seed of man and the nations.

This means that women who have been desiring but unable to have children for years will suddenly become pregnant. God is going to multiply seed in the earth with the intent that righteous parents will raise these children to know the Lord. Early in 1994, I heard a prophecy saying that the majority of the aborted babies in the United States had been male children, progenitors of the seed.

God said in a dramatized word of prophecy that millions of little boys will still be born into the earth. Years ago I spoke through the Holy Spirit that God laughs at the report that the black race in the United States will be wiped out due to abortion, incarcerations and murders of black males (several secular news reports have expressed the seriousness of this real threat). God said there would continue to be seed for the black race, for He created each race for His purpose and good pleasure and none would be destroyed.

God has a purpose for every race, nationality, kindred, tongue and nation. I believe that the Lord has assured me that my son will live to be more than the twenty-five years predicted as the average age limit for the black male. We must carefully and deliberately destroy these evil secular predictions regardless of our race!

We have a promise from God, and He has focused His attention upon the seed, particularly the seed that is in bondage. When Pharaoh began to decimate the male seed of Israel, God sent the Israelites a deliverer. Moses' prophetic acts against Pharaoh and Egypt were so incredibly dramatic that the world still tells the story in each generation. It has even inspired classic literary works and films. Abortion is at an all-time high worldwide, and God, once again, is about to raise up deliverers.

In Somalia recently, we saw thousands of American troops sent to aid the Somalian government. As I watched the news reports of the sending of these troops, I became furious and wept bitterly. "Lord," I cried, "they should have done this a good twenty years ago. It seems some government officials simply do these things for political reasons, just to make themselves look good and not for altruistic reasons."

But the Holy Spirit instantly began to speak to me and said, "No, they could not have sent them twenty years ago. It was not time. Somalia was once a land that knew My name, but fell into idolatry against Me. Therefore, the judgment of the earth came upon them, and the earth itself revolted against them."

He told me that for two hundred years, however, people there have cried out in His name, and in His timing, He sent deliverance through the troops of the United States of America and other foreign nations. At the time only one in every four children was surviving in Somalia, belying the severity of their condition.

God is good, and He is just. If He will do that for a nation that has been into idolatry for hundreds of years in order to raise up seed to His name, He will do the same for idolatrous America, but only if we cry out to Him. For the sake of the righteous, in Somalia, God raised up American men and women of many nationalities, many white, from a nation not yet free from racism, to deliver black babies from death.

Little did we know at the time those troops were dispersed that God was prophetically using those valiant men and women to dramatically demonstrate His word: "Out of Somalia I will yet raise up deliverers." His provision through the U.S. and others is helping to squelch enough of the oppression to aid in bringing this word to pass. Despite the anguish we have seen, God will honor our prayers and actions as catalysts through which He will accomplish His Word.

The Old Testament prophet, Hosea, may have had the most difficult assignment to enact of anyone. (See the book of Hosea.) God, desiring to prophesy to Israel through Hosea's life, told the prophet to go marry a prostitute as a symbol of Israel's "whoredoms."

Hosea not only did it, but later, after his wife left him for other lovers, took her back as a symbol of God's everlasting love and mercy. He had a child by this woman, whose name was Jezreel. Most Bible scholars believe that the "Lo" prefix preceding the other significant prophetic names, implied the later two children were not his but products of his wife's adultery. However, Hosea, in true dramatic style, goes to the marketplace and buys back his wife, now a slave, with silver. The book vividly paints a picture of the entire plan of salvation literally enacted through the life, death and resurrection of Christ Jesus. Hosea's very name means "salvation."

Through the Eyes of the Prophet

Some prophets see visions and have dreams. Some hear the words in their spirit, and others simply speak and hear the words of a prophecy for the first time out of their own mouths. A few people say they actually *see* words, combining visions with speech to prophesy.

Personally, I see detailed pictures. If the picture is a bit hazy, it means whatever is being prophesied is at a distance, and the Lord is hiding something He does not want me to address at that time. The pictures I see may move quickly, forcing me to pay close attention to the details.

Most prophets agree it can be devastating to see things that are not mentionable in public. You may clearly see lust and wickedness in a church service, but the Lord is not willing to allow you to rebuke the person or persons involved.

On the occasions when the prophets are released to bring rebukes or correction, God will direct seasoned prophets to carefully choose their language so as not to devastate its target. It is sometimes quite necessary that the word be laced with His love and concern, drawing the receiver into His purpose. Or perhaps the opposite effect is required of God; that is, to express an action as so distasteful in the sight of God that the receiver vividly hears and understands to cease immediately or suffer the consequences.

A good example: Malachi's words to Israel concerning the treachery of unfounded, unnecessary divorce.

> **Yet you say, "For what reason?" Because the Lord has been witness between you and the wife of your youth, with whom you have dealt treacherously; yet she is your companion and your wife by covenant.**

> **But did He not make them one, having a remnant of the Spirit? And why one? He seeks godly offspring. Therefore take heed to your spirit, and let none deal treacherously with the wife of his youth.**
>
> **"For the Lord God of Israel says that He hates divorce, for it covers one's garment with violence," says the Lord of hosts. "Therefore take heed to your spirit, that you do not deal treacherously."**
>
> **Malachi 2:14-16**

A prophet's mode of delivery must be circumspect and in the will of God.

An experienced, sensitive prophet will know when it is necessary to pull a person aside for whom he has a word that might be embarrassing or incriminating if given in public. Usually, he will ask one or more of the church leaders to witness the word, so that the person is not undone before the entire congregation.

There may be a few times when God will have a prophet deliver a stinging rebuke in Old Testament style, but He immediately will begin to replace what was stripped away with His will. After God does surgery, He pours oil in the place where something was removed.

God only sends a rebuke as a warning that someone is in danger of jeopardizing something in his relationship with God. Or God is attempting to move a person into a deeper relationship with Himself. He never brings a rebuke for the purpose of condemnation, which is unprofitable.

Personally, the only times I have ever seen God give a prophet license to openly chastise someone has been when that person is in a life and death or destructive situation and will not hear the word of the Lord any other way.

The Depth of Anointing

The mode of delivery, however, does not measure the depth of the prophet nor does it measure the depth of the content of the prophecy. In other words, *how* a prophecy is delivered does not always determine *how serious* it is, nor is the mode of delivery always an indication of the spirituality of the prophet.

Spiritual depth comes from these things:

1. The degree, or measure, of the Word in the spirit of the prophet.
2. How consecrated his life is before the Lord.
3. The measure of faith in which the prophet operates.
4. The measure of yieldedness in the prophet's life.
5. The strength of the prophet's prayer life.

There are diversities of prophetic anointings, just as there are diverse styles, or modes, of delivery. However, these diversities are only designed by God to enhance, helping the words spoken to appeal to all people in a way they can accept and understand. They are not given to provoke jealousy, envy, or covetousness, but to mutually benefit God's prized possession, His bride.

All prophets flow as individuals, but should be flexible enough to minister in teams or companies. Prophets set the pace for how God desires to flow in a given service or place. They often reveal and expose the hidden plots of the enemy.

A divine flow of prophecy will not violate, but will enhance God's purpose, becoming a vehicle of fulfillment. A divine flow may leave room for other yielded parties to enter in (1 Sam. 10:10,11; 1 Cor. 14:31,33), though they may not be prophets at all.

A most important factor in the mode of delivery is timing. As I have mentioned several times, the Bible says **the spirits of the prophets are subject to the prophets** (1 Cor. 14:32). That means the prophet can hold his peace until the proper time. Whatever prophetic word comes to your spirit is under your control as God directs the timing of its delivery.

It has been necessary for me to hold words of prophecy for protracted periods of time, until the Lord decreed, "Speak." On one occasion, I had a word for a particular pastor that took two years almost to the day I received it before I could deliver it. God's reasoning was that the pastor was not open to receive it until then. Therefore, two years of intercession had to precede the delivery of the word so that God's will could be accomplished. If it had been given prematurely, the opposite effect from God's intention may have happened.

Within that period of intercession, the pastor became a broken, yielded man. His marriage, then broken, was restored. His congregation, formerly devastated, was reforming, this time healthily. By the time the word was released, everything was in place for it to be received, causing that house to experience a glorious transformation.

Other Questions Concerning Prophecy

There are several questions that are frequently asked me at seminars and services when I teach on prophets and prophecy.

One of the most common is, "Should not prophecy always bear witness in the spirit of the intended for it to be of God?"

This is commonly taught by many people, that the criteria for judging the accuracy of a prophecy is whether or not it "witnesses" to you. As I shared in an earlier testimony, it is certainly not necessary for prophecy to bear witness for it to be of God. Several scriptural examples come to mind.

Ahab the king is given a prophecy by Micaiah the prophet, who foretells Ahab's death on the battlefield. This prophecy was rejected by Ahab to the extent that he not only would not cancel the battle, but he foolishly disguised himself so as not to draw attention to the fact that he was king. He died on the battlefield after randomly being struck by an arrow. If he had believed the prophet, he would have repented and prospered. (1 Kings 22.)

The scripture says that Sarah laughed when the angel prophesied to her that she would bear a child in her old age (Gen. 18:12). But after the creative word was spoken, Hebrews 11:11,17-20 speaks of this miracle coming to pass by her faith, and that of her convinced husband, Abraham.

The prophecy of Saul becoming the first king of Israel so bore witness with Saul that on coronation day he was hiding with the baggage. God had to change his heart to prepare him for the task. (1 Sam. 10.)

It is often taught that a prophecy will not give direction or guidance but only *confirm* something you already know from God.

However, if we take the Old Testament example of Naaman, we can see that this is not always the case. Naaman, a Syrian general, was told by Elisha's messenger to dip seven times in the Jordan to be healed of leprosy. (2 Kings 5:1-19.)

Naaman certainly had no witness to what Elisha's messenger said. The Jordan was a muddy, swiftly flowing river in most places. Syria had a number of clear, clean, beautiful streams and rivers. Why could he not dip into them?

His little Israelite slave girl talked him into it, saying, "What have you got to lose?"

When he did what the prophet said, Naaman found out that the word of the Lord to him was true. He was very grateful.

Some things you hear prophetically may not bear witness at all in your spirit at the time, yet they may be true.

Although it is true that possibly most of the prophecy you will receive will be confirmational, this is not a rule of thumb. Prophecy does not *have* to be confirmational.

The second most asked question is, "How does one receive prophecy?"

You receive prophecy by opening your spirit to hear the voice of God. However, it is not God's best for you to constantly seek out prophets to give you a word. The best way is to seek God for His will in your life through prayer, fasting and studying His Word. If He wants to give you a special word, He can see to it that a prophet finds you. There are instances when it is acceptable to seek out a prophet. However, this should not be a pattern of life for anyone. God said man cannot live by bread alone, but by every word that proceeds out of the mouth of God, not out of the mouth of the prophet.

Another misnomer is that receiving a lot of personal prophecy means that you cannot hear from God for yourself. Perhaps some people get more prophecies than others because they are in a better position to receive more often, or are more yielded, or perhaps require more public acknowledgement. Though there are many reasons for this phenomena, the least of them is an inability to hear God.

The ultimate "word of the Lord" for all of us has already been given. It is the Bible.

You receive prophecy in the spirit in which it is intended. It may be for edification, comfort, or exhortation, sent to build or call you into your full purpose in God. It may be given to assure you that your prayers are being answered. Perhaps it will confirm your healing, physically, emotionally, or spiritually.

Prophecy should always, first and foremost, be immediately given back to God, whether you feel a witness or not. If He is the real giver, He will return it with understanding of its meaning at the proper time. While prophets are given intuitive interpretive skills, most personal words are not to be interpreted back to individuals beyond what God has expressed as the sentiment of the word. Each prophet should have an excellent witness in spirit as to God's intent, but is not required by Him to interpret the when, where, or how of prophecies beyond that sensing.

It is not just the prophet who must ascertain God's timing. The person receiving a prophecy must also seek God as to when this thing is to be. One well-known teacher in the Body tells of hearing God tell him that he would send him to a South American country. The man sold his house and got ready to go, but nothing ever happened.

Fifteen years later, he was in that country, having totally forgotten about the prophecy, when God suddenly spoke to him and said, "This is what I was talking about fifteen years ago."

A third question I am asked is this: "Are 'words' amounting to generalities which are given in services really prophecies?"

Once a woman arose in a service and spoke in tongues for about fifteen minutes. Her interpretation was:

"Ohhh, ohhh, sin, sin, sin. Sin in the camp, sin in the camp. God says there is sin in the camp." That was the gist of her prophetic word.

Another gentleman once prophesied that we (the congregation) were pleasing to God and that He desired we come closer to Him in the Spirit. He used many words to say it, but that was basically all that was said.

Both are examples of what is called exhortation. Exhortations need not be preceded by "thus saith the Lord."

Much of what is accepted in the church as prophecy is simple exhortation. It is not prophetic at all. These kinds of "prophecies" also may be nothing but exhibitionism, a desire on the part of the person giving them to be noticed or accepted. But regardless of the intent, the fact is, they do not constitute prophecy.

Another explanation for generalized prophecies is that the prophet, or person prophesying, has remained in one area of revelation and not continued to move on with the Lord. When I was a young Christian, most of the prophecies I heard were like this: "Yea, My children, draw nigh unto Me, and I'll draw nigh unto you. Yea, I will carry your burden for you. I will lift you up." The theme was always to bring comfort.

I could mouth the words along with them, because I knew what would be said. In certain other circles, prophecies would always have "blessings of abundance" themes.

If you only focus on one area of the Word of God, you are only going to be able to prophesy out of that area. You cannot go beyond your own knowledge and understanding of the things of God. A prophet proficient in the Word of God has a rich vocabulary of the Spirit stored for God's use.

8
Case Histories: True and False Prophets

Throughout this book, I have given some examples of true and false prophecies, believing one of the best *modes* of teaching is through examples. Therefore, I want to give you more illustrations of prophetic people and how to recognize the true from the false. To start, here is an example of a prophecy my husband, George, and I received with which we had absolutely no witness at all!

Prophet Bernard Jordan of Brooklyn, New York, called us one morning weeks after we'd first met. Later, we developed a closer relationship, but at the time, we did not know each other well. He said the Holy Spirit had told him to call us, and he proceeded to give us a startlingly specific and accurate word.

Within the prophecy God spoke through Bernard, he said that George would be involved in the '88 national elections into the 90s. At that point, George was not even registered to vote in the state of Oklahoma where we resided. In addition to that, my father had been involved in Republican politics all of my life. I'd suffered some very unpleasant experiences because of it, and I hated the political arena.

This prophecy not only did not confirm anything *to* us, it did not bear witness in us at all! But being fairly knowledgeable by then about prophecy, we both knew not to discard or treat it lightly as if untrue just because it did not bear witness. Instead, we did what everyone should do in such a case: We gave it back to God, with proper attention in prayer. In the end, we received that it was from God, although we did not understand it.

In 1987, Pat Robertson became a presidential candidate and through a series of circumstances, George was asked to take the position of regional press secretary over eleven states. However, a second prophecy concerning his involvement in the campaign revealed he would become national press secretary. Still, George was a bit incredulous at Marilyn Price, his personal secretary's prediction, but as God would have it, he became the national press secretary. That meant he was not only involved in the '88 elections as Jordan had said, but presently he still receives calls related to the political arena, based on that experience.

Neither prophecy bore witness when given, but both turned out to be the word of the Lord, coming to pass in detail.

Witchcraft Can Masquerade as Prophetic

In the years that I have been involved in prophetic ministry, I have become acquainted with several situations of a peculiar, bizarre nature. I have known false prophets or apostles, both male and female, who have found weaker, younger Christians to dominate in a twisted, perverted manner. Several such incidents developed into unusually wicked sexual perversions, resulting in the calling up of ancient historical sex demons (incubus and sucubus). These "spirit" partners would commit lewd sexual acts with the "would be" prophets. In one incredible case, spiritual husbands were conjured up through "prayer" to facilitate the waiting prophetic wives.

Another common thread in this fake tapestry is that the stronger forces the weaker to become the prophet spokesman. In the event that a rebuke or correction is ministered, the false prophet hides behind the skirts of the weaker spokesman, going undetected for their part in the deception.

Also common to each incident was the overwhelming usurping of authority over the other in the name of the Lord. Prophecy became the end for every directive. One precious saint, after having fallen prey to a false prophet, drank Lysol in an effort to purge her system in preparation for fasting. After almost dying, God managed to speak to her spirit to receive help to escape the bondage.

There have actually been witchcraft practitioners who, in the name of prophecy, held entire churches in captivity. One such person came to a church in a small town under the guise of an apostle. The man taught such errant doctrine that it split the church in fragments. Many years later, this religious philosophy that demeans women is still dividing churches — in God's name!

Witchcraft and rebellion are the same in the sight of God. (1 Sam. 15:23.) It is not His intention for the Church to disallow or disavow the prophetic because of the false. However, it is the duty of the eldership elect to work in conjunction with the prophet to stop the Church from being infiltrated by such blatant acts of demonic invasion. (1 Cor. 12:1,4,12,25.) The first step is to realize that no one, within themselves, is above being fooled. We need the strength and unity of the brethren uniting together to expose the undercover works of the enemy. Usually, these who fall prey, becoming totally deceived, are lone wolves.

Don't be fooled! If you believe you are legitimately called to some status in the prophetic, submit yourself first to God and then to the authorities He creates as His agents to perfect those things concerning you. Everyone should have someone who can speak wisdom and/or correction into their lives. If we would conduct ourselves in this manner, there would be few incidents of false ministers destroying innocent lambs throughout the Body.

Several years ago in the American Church, women began to gather together as intercessors for local churches and ministries. Much good was accomplished, yet in some of these groups such things as the above illustrations began to surface. Something that may have started as a creative idea given to one person was twisted out of context and spread as wildfire.

More godless acts were committed in these prayer meetings or came out of them than many pastors want to realize. Was it a bad thing for women to meet for prayer? Absolutely not! Was it a bad thing for them to meet without a spiritual covering? Yes! That is how the intercession movement got off base and began to give prophetic ministry a bad name.

Today, many pastors and denominations want to throw out the baby with the bath water, so to speak, because of situations such as this. They do not want to hear of prophecy, the gifts of the Spirit, or any other supernatural movement of God.

I know of another woman in my hometown who received a prophecy that she was to leave her husband, sell her beautiful home and brand new furniture and get rid of her new automobile. She was told that God had said she was involved in "an illegal union" with her husband, who was not saved.

She was to leave him, sell everything and God would open a door to send her to a foreign nation as a missionary. She followed this prophecy, lost everything she had, and to my knowledge, never went on the mission field. After suffering for seven or eight months, she pulled herself together and got a job. However, to this day — many years later — she has not fully recovered.

Much damage can be done through false prophecy. However, I want to make it clear that there is absolutely nothing wrong or inappropriate about gathering together and praying. Christians *should* and *must* meet together and pray regularly. The danger comes when people begin to prophesy over one another without any proper oversight from spiritual elders.

If you are in a place where that begins to frequently happen, leave because it is a potentially dangerous place to be. I know of a group in Tulsa who came together to pray and right now are believing God told them to stand in faith for the return of spouses who left them *and are remarried.*

It is of the utmost necessity that we become totally immersed in God's Word, in prayer and a consecrated lifestyle, for the Bible warns that evil spirits will seduce and deceive even the elect, if possible. (Mark 13:22.) You need not fear unclean spirits if you remain in the shelter of God's tender care.

Psychic Is Not Prophetic or Spiritual

Many of these false operations and manifestations are occurring in the world, which is accepting all stratas of supernatural phenomena as "psychic." After seeing what is being published and what is on television and in films, we should not be surprised at this. However, we need to understand that the same false and counterfeit signs and wonders can, and are, happening within the Church.

I have prayed for people who have operated under a demonic anointing. I have met people who did psychic healing, and there is much documented evidence as to these healings, just as there is to healings manifested by the Holy Spirit. Increasingly more every day, we are seeing the subtle, steady introduction of psychics, witchcraft and the supernatural being inducted into every facet of human life. This leaves gaping, wide doors of entrance to false prophets and socially acceptable demonic behavior.

One partial definition of a false prophet is someone who may potentially be called to prophesy, but does not have a relationship with the Giver of prophecy, Jesus Christ. They enter into the supernatural illegally, not by the blood of Jesus. The so-called prophets in the preceding illustrations were all false. But what is to be pitied is that each felt they were serving God!

I know of a woman who travels the Body of Christ to this day, ministering in large meetings. She was caught going into pastors' offices to look for names and addresses to use in order to call people out during her meetings. Of course, she would get enough responses to look authentic, justifying her false prophetic call by acquired knowledge.

That kind of "charlatanry" is going on throughout the Church, and you can be fooled if you are not careful to know what the Bible says for yourself. Those who are greedy will be seduced by such a spirit also, but the pure in heart God will protect.

You can know the workings of a familiar spirit by the fact that it only draws attention to what is familiar around a person with no apparent reason or outcome. Then it seals its seduction by promising some fortunate prize that may never be acquired. It flatters only for the gain of its procurers, but in the end, it will rape both the vessel used and its target.

If ever there was a generation that needed understanding about the prophetic, it is this one. Prophets are needed to judge the words of other prophets (1 Cor. 14:29) so that innocent babes will not be undone by the false and can learn to appreciate the true.

Of course, there could be no false if there were not first a true to be imitated. I have been in gatherings where prophets have prophesied so specifically and accurately that everyone was visibly moved.

I particularly remember being at a women's conference seeing and hearing a certain prophetess dramatically illustrate the word of the Lord to a minister of the church. The prophetess pushed the woman moderately hard once, then very hard a second time, causing the woman to be knocked to the floor. The word came saying that the enemy had come to destroy, literally beating her and knocking her to the ground, repeatedly. But, God would shortly show her a door of escape, and when to go through the door. From there He would minister His healing to her broken heart and wounded spirit, making her totally whole. The woman dissolved in tears as God's healing began in her. It was later learned that her husband had been physically abusive. The word of a true prophet ministers life.

I have had many such testimonies of expressly accurate prophecies given to me over the years. In 1980, a close friend and prophetess, Nettie Jones, drove across town to my home to deliver a prophetic warning and blessing.

She had been in intercession for me when God spoke to her that His desire was for me to marry, but I was paying no attention to the young men I was meeting in my travels. (I was not married at the time.) She said very plainly, "One of these young men is your husband. You will meet him at a Full Gospel Business Men's Convention. He is about six feet tall, very intelligent and committed to the Kingdom. However, if you don't stop being so very shy, you will miss this man. You will come to know him in '82 and marry in '83."

Another prophetess, Shirley McKinney, of Cleveland, Ohio, gave me a similar word concerning marriage saying she saw a tall, brown-skinned man with a scar on the right cheek. Both confirmed that the man was not from my hometown.

In 1979, I actually met George Vinnett, my husband, briefly. In 1981, I saw him once again while traveling, but on neither occasion did we talk more than five minutes. And both meetings were at Full Gospel Business Men's Conventions. However, in 1982, a mutual friend asked George to call my father on ministry business, and I answered the phone. This began a wonderful friendship that resulted in marriage June 18, 1983, just as the prophetess spoke. My husband suffered an auto accident in April, 1966, leaving a noticeable scar on his right cheek. Many of the other things, too numerous to mention concerning our calls together, are still happening to this very day.

It is more important than ever to know how to discern the true from the false, because I believe we are living in an age when prophets like Jeremiah or Agabus will literally go into the White House and prophesy to the President. In fact, I know of one who already has done so.

There will be confrontations between psychic powers and the prophets of God, and the devil will lose every time. God may be laughing but He is not joking in this move. He is sitting in the heavenlies and laughing at the calamity of those who say He does not exist, or who say there are many avenues to get to Him other than through the blood of His Son, Jesus. (Ps. 2:4,5.)

We are living in very exciting times. I believe God is going to defend His Church as never before. The early apostles who established the Church longed to see the day in which we are privileged to live.

It will be exciting to see how God is going to close the final chapters of His saga, for the end of many things as we know them is now upon us. Look to the heavens, and observe the times. The guard is fast changing.

9
The Changing of the Guard

The return of the Lord Jesus Christ is, of course, nearer than ever in the history of the Church or the world. Most of us who await His coming are so greatly anticipating His arrival that we are beginning to long for it. Scripture supports the fact that this longing, or feeling of imminence, is quite natural to the committed believer. Indeed the Apostle Paul and his contemporaries all felt this way. The danger is when we become so overtaken with His return that we lose our sense of urgency to tell the uninformed masses that He came the first time

I remember actually having an argument with the Lord concerning the rapture (1 Thess. 4:13-18) and His Kingdom. He spoke to my spirit very clearly. "You are not Kingdom-minded. If you were, you would be interceding for your children's future spouses, and you would be praying now for their ministries when they are grown." God read the selfish desire of my heart that did not want to think long range into the future. My heart, instead, was fixed on His near return to the extent that I hoped my children would not be here long enough to marry! Jesus said that we should occupy until He returns. (Luke 19:13.) His greatest concern is for the earth to be prepared for His coming, and that preparation can only be accomplished by the Church. Our assignment is to advance the Kingdom, taking the truth to every nation.

On another occasion, as I was giving an altar call, the Holy Spirit responded to my appeal by saying, "I never told you that." What was He referring to? My saying to the audience, "If you were the *only* one, Christ would have died for you." Needless to say, I was convicted and quite shocked. But when I faced reality, I clearly saw that I had picked up the terminology from other ministers who rightly sounded spiritual when using it. For them, it was revelation and yet for me it was mere mimicry. I asked God to reveal what distressed Him about my usage of the phrase. He said, "For those to whom I'm sending you, this will instill a selfish mentality. The people will look at salvation as being for them and no one else. The truth is, I would not have died for one, for I came in the fullness of time to get them *all*."

It is more than possible that many of us who are sensing the Lord's coming are actually sensing this next move. If we don't realize the move is already in progress, we may be missing the greatest move of God ever.

Whenever God begins to bring a new move of restoration, there is a time of transition, a time of restlessness and turmoil, between the old and the new. Of course, whenever God strategically begins His move, the enemy counters in an attempt to arrest the efforts of God and the Church. In the Bible and in Church history, we see that he has had varying success, depending upon how God's people received His latest movement.

God expressed to me many years ago that He was not troubled at all with our labeling His movements. Labels are for men to accurately describe how God is moving. However, God does have a problem when we encamp in the move we have named. In Genesis 1, God began to move, and there is no indication anywhere in Scripture that He has ceased.

The Enemies of a New Move

Every facet of God's Kingdom has its own unique provisions. But with every advancement of God's army comes a well armed barrage by demonic henchmen, whose sole plan is to stop the advancement. Although there are many more of Satan's tactics that could be listed, I will highlight only nine of his most destructive weapons.

The first three "weapons" of the enemy are:

1. The old guard, or the leaders who refuse to advance.

2. The religious "sanhedrin" of the day, or those locked into doctrines and traditions.

3. Heresies, or false beliefs and doctrines. These are things which divert the attention of the Body away from God's directives.

The "old guard," or the leaders of the old move, often do not see the validity of the new move, nor recognize its leadership. Church history will attest to the fact that every new move of God has had its chief protesters among the old guard. But God's tactical plan for those of the prior order is to have them help the next generation make the transition gracefully. They are to accomplish this by depositing into the next generation all of the truth which God has deposited in them. There should be no intimidation or resentment, nor fear of being replaced, but a healthy respect for God's choice and a recognition of the extremely important role of the old guard toward the new.

I believe if any generation is capable of ending the trend of intimidation between the old and the new, it is this one. It must be realized that there is actually nothing wrong with the old guard; it is simply time for the new generation to change the mode of advancement.

Of course, some will be replaced because of pride, greed, or other vices, lest they become like King Saul when he surmised David would replace him. He was not only jealous of David but fearful, and came to hate him. His attitude allowed an evil spirit to come upon him that drove him to try to murder David.

Jesus said you cannot put new wine in old wine bottles. (Matt. 9:17.) It is an exceptional Christian who can make the transition through several moves, incorporating into his life what is good and laying aside the things which are off center with each move. There are a few spiritual leaders who have done this, but not enough.

We even see the example of the old versus the new in Jesus' day. The Pharisees, the religious right and the Sadducees, leaders of the old way, were His chief antagonists, though the common people adored Him. The pattern repeats itself throughout history. Those of the previous move "stone" those of the next.

But the leadership of the present move not only has the opportunity but also the equipment to help facilitate a smooth transition. They must not allow religiosity or any other false concept to obstruct their vision. Being carried away with the view that our way is the best and only way, qualifies one for the religious sanhedrin of the day. Those who sit on this council generally have enough of the crowd and financial resources to seriously hinder transition. However, the one thing that the sanhedrin never reckons with is the fact that God simply will not be stopped. The persecution only pressed Jesus deeper into purpose and will do the same for us, if we allow it.

With each Kingdom advancement, the enemy's victories should become fewer and fewer as God increases in the midst of His Body. But we may still see the greater move come in this generation as a result of the obvious placement of the apostle and the prophet. Identifying and mobilizing the Church to destroy these satanic tactics is all a part of the call of these peculiar officers. Satan will only increase his seditious plays, but God's people will finally awaken to them and stop joining him en masse.

Warring factions, religious views, zeal (not according to knowledge, Rom. 10:2), and pride are chief factors in the preaching of heretical doctrines. Ignorance of the truth concerning God's Word acts as a hot bed for these kinds of falsehoods. And, what is criminal is that innocent, well-meaning members spread the good-sounding, ear-tickling fallacies much like a highly contagious disease.

How can we identify and stop heresies? How can we keep from accepting doctrines and traditions of men as current revelation and truth? By learning and knowing the Word of God and the God of His Word for ourselves. When all of the ministries of God, particularly the apostles, prophets and teachers, begin **rightly dividing the word of truth** (2 Tim. 2:15), there will start to be an end to the rampant heresies that always precede new moves. With God's strength, we can put away these works of the flesh and become steadfast, for this is an absolute necessity in the next move. (Gal. 5:15-21.)

Six More Ways the Enemy Hinders a New Move

It is not always pleasant to endure transition. However, if you observe the season, discerning the times, transition can be quite exciting. The Church has been undergoing massive transition for more than a decade.

These years have been exciting, though not always pleasant. It seems we have had greater opposition to this move than any prior move. This one is pregnant with the meat of the truth of every prior move. It just stands to reason Satan's tactics would increase. Even in our personal spiritual lives, it has seemed as though we are being challenged in *everything* we have ever believed about God. The world and Satan are asking hard, probing questions. But, the good news is that we really are advancing forward and with answers to hard inquiries our immediate predecessors never dreamed of facing. We are demanded to give an account of the hope that is within us. (1 Pet. 3:15.)

We have seen three ways the devil challenges in these times. The fourth, and for many ministers the greatest enemy, is *discouragement*.

Once again, we will look at the life of Elijah, who represents the early order of the apostle and, of course, prophet. He ministered with great signs and wonders. Elijah was considered the greatest prophet ever until the coming of John the Baptist, according to Jesus' words. In fact, Jesus speaking of John, refers to him as Elias (Elijah) who was to come. (Matt. 11:14.) He spoke to heads of state and common people alike. Yet this tremendous man of God fell prey to this fourth ploy of the enemy. He allowed himself to fall into discouragement.

While on a missions trip to Singapore early in 1994, I ministered to delegates from thirteen nations. I poured myself out to such an extent that I lost weight as a result of the Holy Spirit moving through me in a powerful display of God's love toward the people.

However, I came home to find that my mother had been hospitalized, this time for the last time. I called to talk with her every day. My father told me later that she was not lucid or able to talk to visitors much of that time, but when I called, she always knew me, knew what I was doing, and asked pertinent questions. She let me pray for her and uplift her in the Lord every time.

During the last days of Mother's life, our church held its annual Azusa Conference in Tulsa, and I was part of a prophetic presbytery. This was the first Azusa with such a presbytery. A total of about twenty thousand people partook of the services during that week. The day before I ministered prophetically to that convention, I talked to my mother for the last time.

She said, "Pam, it is not going to happen the way we all have wanted it to. Mother won't be healed this time. Jesus already has visited me, and I am going home. Rejoice, for mine is going to be a glorious death. This is not a sad occasion. This is good news. Something wonderful is about to happen to your mama!"

I said, "Mama, do you want me to come home?"

And I will never forget her words as long as I live.

She said, "No, what you are doing is too important. Don't vacate your post on the wall. (Nehemiah 6:3 expresses this concept of not being diverted.) Stay there."

Then she prophesied that my children would all grow up to be tremendous warriors of God with great ministries. She also felt that she would be able to see this from the grandstand of the heavenlies, that somehow God had assured her that she would. (Heb. 12:1.)

She said, "I'm ready to go. I've run my course, and I'm through with this life. Just pray that God will help me with the transition by helping me to understand why I am making the change in this way."

That night we ministered the Word of God to a great body of believers, and the following morning my mother went into glory. I can truly say now that some things can be discouraging to the point of despair. This was, beyond a doubt, the hardest trial I have ever had to face.

My mother and I were so incredibly close. We shared continually. I will always miss her. Dr. Norman Wagner, her pastor in Youngstown, preached her eulogy, "A Greater Than Miriam Was Here." His powerful message was that Mother's anointing was from Christ; therefore, her administration was greater than that of Miriam, the sister of Moses, whose anointing preceded the coming of Jesus.

This period of my life marked the greatest challenge I have had in every area of faith. Though I knew a full month ahead that she was going to die, when it actually came time to release her, it was just as difficult as if I had not known. In fact, were it not for God's supreme love and grace for all of the family, this would have been virtually impossible.

I began to question everything I believed concerning God, Mother and my call: Was there a Heaven? Does God really heal anyone anymore today, since He did not do it for Mother? If I am really a prophet, why was I not able to prevent this death? How can psychics seem to do some of the same things prophets do in the Lord? Why do so many of the righteous die all too soon, when some wicked seem to live long, prosperous lives?

If you've never experienced this oppression, I assure you that, regardless of your strength and knowledge of God, the enemy will attempt to overwhelm you!

It is as though you became delirious for a fraction of eternity. Time stands still as you contend with spirits in the greatest of battlefields: the mind. But this is not an amazing trial in the sight of God. Jesus experienced the exact same kind of attack over and over in the Scriptures, from the temptation in the wilderness to the agony of the cross. (Luke 4:1-13; John 19:25-30; Ps. 22:1-21.) Yet He triumphed over principalities to allow us the same privilege and ability. So though the attacks seem overwhelming and incredulous, you can overcome.

I know what it is like to be bombarded with discouragement, but God is ever faithful. At my mother's funeral, I sang, danced and testified of the power of God and the unforgettable contribution Mother made to the Body and to our Father God. Then I returned to Tulsa and finished the course for my school of ministry. God fights discouragement in us by and through His Word. But we must see the design of the enemy and pick up the sword to fight along with the Father. (Eph. 6:10-17.)

Every time those thoughts came to mind, the Word of the Lord became stronger. Now I feel that I can aptly say, "Lord, I know what I believe and don't know how *not* to believe in You." I have greater courage than ever before and am able to deal with obstacles that previously would have been my undoing. Though I am not so high-minded as to think I have arrived at my zenith, I am so grateful to be aware of God's enormous capacity to inject durability into the believer.

In 1 Kings 18 and 19, the Prophet Elijah experienced a similar kind of discouragement directly following what seemed to be his greatest victory. He literally called down fire from heaven to consume a sopping-wet sacrifice, after which he slew 450 false prophets. However, when threatened by the wicked matriarch, Jezebel, Elijah ran fearing his life would be forfeited to the witch.

Discouraged, he requested God take away his life, as he had no more power than his forefathers against the rulers of darkness. (v. 4.) But God would not permit Elijah to remain despondent. Instead, just as with you and me, God addressed the discouragement in four distinct ways.

1. He showed Elijah his purpose, to call kings or God's chosen into their future and to set the order of Israel (the Church) through the prophetic.

2. God gave Elijah a successor, Elisha, contending that he had a relevant future. (v. 16.)

3. He reminded him of his promises and showed Elijah he was not alone. (v. 18.)

4. God assured Elijah that He was not in the hurricane winds, the earthquake, nor the fire. (v. 12.)

The winds of adversity seemed overwhelming, as well as the shaking of the foundation of all Elijah believed to be true. As though this was not enough, a fire seemingly threatened to devour all of the works previously established by Elijah and his predecessors. (vv. 11,12.) God proved to Elijah He was not in the wind, the earthquake, or the fire, but in a still, small voice only heard in intimacy. By so doing, God utterly destroyed Elijah's discouragement for the remainder of his days. Enduring and overcoming adversity in God strengthens our reserve.

The fifth tactic of the enemy is the *threat of death,* either natural or the death of a God-given vision. In 1 Samuel 22:11-19, King Saul commanded the death of eighty-five priests of God because they had assisted David, God's new choice to rule in Israel.

I believe that today we will be pressed with the threat of death on all sides and placed in a position to stand up for what we believe. Persecution will gravely increase. We must become so secure in what we believe that no fear of death will cause us to lose the victory.

A sixth enemy of a new move is *moral failure.* The devil often covertly sets traps for believers in any area he can detect a weakness. I have never heard of as many ministers falling into moral failure as I have in this generation. It should come as no surprise, for television, movies, stage plays and literature have subtly inundated society with decadence over the years. The enemy has slyly deadened our senses to seeing sin in the hope that the anesthetic will also not prevent us from committing sin. Scripture warns that this effect of repeated sin is the same as having the conscience seared as with a hot iron. (1 Tim. 4:1,2.)

Moral failure begins in the heart before it eve becomes an act of betrayal against God. (Gen. 34:2.) God will no longer accept "unclean" sacrifices, any more than He did with Eli's sons. I believe God is searching for those with clean hearts and hands to consistently and faithfully handle the anointing in this next move.

A minister once told me that thoughts of adultery came into his mind, and he read where Jesus said that *looking* upon a woman in lust was the same as committing adultery. (Matt. 5:28.) Deducing that he had already committed adultery in his mind, instead of repenting, he went out and committed the act of adultery! That may sound ridiculous and even stupid to some of us, yet there are Christians all over the world doing the same kinds of things. The greatest deterrent to moral failure is a renewed mind and consistent, intimate fellowship with the Lord. (Rom. 12:1,2.) Every member of the Body must be careful to carry themselves with integrity.

The seventh tactic, similar to the sixth, is *an unrepentant heart.* Far too many people are indulging in secret sins and have done so until their hearts are hardened. They literally no longer feel convicted over their sins, bearing little or no godly sorrow. If they are in the ministry, and God has continued to allow His anointing to manifest through them, this may be mistaken for His condoning their immoral behavior. This is a fallacy, which all will find out. It is also extremely dangerous. (Rom. 1.)

Even more deadly in the sight of God is one who never repents until actually caught. Sunday after Sunday altar calls are flooded with teary-eyed "repenters," half of whom are only saying, "God, I'm so very sorry You caught me." True repentance means to turn away from sin, never to return. (John 8:10,11.) You may not immediately feel the effects of sin, for it is first pleasing, then easy and then guiltless.

You must become aware of what dangerous ground you tread upon if your conscience no longer pricks you for sinning. God may even manifest in you for a certain period of time only known to Him, just as with Samson. But in the end, you will suffer a deadly penalty, as Samson did, for his transgression.

Occasionally falling into sin is one thing. God has made provision for it through the atonement of Jesus. (1 John 2:1.) However, *willfully* and repeatedly sinning (or transgressing) after coming to the knowledge of the truth says to Jesus, "Your blood is not powerful enough to deliver me from my sin. It is simply too difficult for me to stop." You place yourself in a position for eternal damnation, for there is no more sacrifice for you. (Heb. 6:4-8.)

The eighth tactic of the enemy is the *mishandling of people, resources and money.* I will not discuss this at length, because everyone has seen this exposed within these last years. The important thing for you to know is that God will no longer permit His most precious commodity to be abused, and that is innocent sheep.

It is expressly important for us to understand that a high moral standard in leadership flows from the head down upon every member, just as the anointing flowed through Aaron's beard, even falling upon his feet. (Ps. 133:1,2.) However, the scenario of wickedness filtering down also is very dramatically displayed through corrupt standards being permitted by those who rule over us.

In the decade of the 90s, we have more than ever as the Church, taken the posture that change is better than good conscience, and leaders should be chosen not by a biblical standard, but upon public policy. We, in turn, said the same thing before God, that Israel expressed when it demanded a king. (1 Sam. 8:6.) We cried, "We want change," and enough of the house of God voted for change for God to make a decision to grant it. We elected a high official who admitted to having an adulterous affair for years, did not deny involvement in anti-war demonstrations against the U.S. in foreign countries, evaded the draft and smoked marijuana (though he did not inhale!). The word even circled within the Body that this "presidential hopeful" was born again, making it palatable for those desiring change to vote change in. Though morality cannot be voted in or legislated, God's desire is for us to observe what is happening around about us and act according to how His Word addresses it. The truth is, because so much of the Church voted yes, an outpouring of unclean spirits was released upon the nation, the same perverse spirits that were at work in the headship.

My aim here is not to unlawfully (by God's standards) criticize the heads of the nation, but to show the awesome spread of wickedness that flows through any group whose headship contains corruption. This nation, allegedly established on God's principles, has for too long allowed unrighteousness to reign. God blames the Church! We must live by a high enough standard that we become the standard by which the world is judged. We must realize that the guard is most emphatically changing, and that we are being given an opportunity to set the standard for the new guard, first in the Church, then in the world. We must live up to our responsibility in every way, whether in the voting booth or in the house of God. And a commitment to prayer for *all* leadership is our answer, coupled with a vow to God that we will abstain from even the appearance of evil (1 Thess. 5:22), much less giving in to moral failure.

The ninth and final enemy is *missing the time of our visitation.* Luke 13:34,35 says that Jesus desired to comfort Jerusalem as a hen gathers her brood, but they would not. He prophesied the desolation of the house of Israel, and it is still happening just as He said it would. God is moving upon us in an amazing time of transition, but it will go by us if we do not realize what season we are in.

The Apostle Paul and his generation longed to see the move of God we are being privileged to see. We have indeed come full circle and are having an opportunity to see all of the five-fold officers in place and to see the Church functioning in her fullest potential. But this can only be accomplished through dedication to prayer, fasting and unwavering faith.

These nine things I have listed are not the only things that develop in opposition to God's new move, but they are among the most common and deadly.

As I said at the onset, God began to move upon the earth in Genesis 1:1 and has never stopped. He operates by perpetually moving forward, despite the fact that we identify His movements for our own sakes. This does not disturb Him, as long as we continue to move with Him. We must not err by thwarting His movement!

How To Be Part of a New Move

I am going to continue to refer to the various aspects of God's moving from Genesis to Revelation as "moves," because that is the way we perceive what He does. However, it will help you to keep in mind that God does not stop and start but is moving in a continuous progression toward His goal.

If you desire to be part of what we perceive God is doing in our time, avoid the nine traps of the enemy I have mentioned.

There is no need for the old guard to resist what God is doing due to their traditions. We must consider that if we are not presently of the old guard, should Jesus tarry, we will also have the experience of becoming the old. When you reach that day, don't allow anything to keep you from properly impacting the younger generation. Deposit all that is within you into them, bringing them into greatness and excellence. Their ministry should far exceed yours, lest you fail in God's commission.

If you are part of the new move, be aware that pride is a chief destructive force that would support harsh criticism of your fathers. We must revere and respect those of the previous move and lift them up before the Lord, that the transition might be smooth and fruitful.

Perhaps you may see a leader's infallibility, new or old guard. Your role as a follower is *not* to judge or correct, but to realize that leadership is corrected from the top down, and not from the general congregation up. If you feel wronged as a congregant, follow the guidelines as set out in 1 Timothy 5:1,2,19. God, through the leader's peers, will usually approach that leader in a scriptural manner. Of course, everyone must first go to God concerning the problem, and then leave the settling or resolution of it to Him. His decisions are always wise and capable of bringing His desired results.

Above all, please do not become religious, falling prey to spirits of legalism, pride and judgment.

Immorality, greed, or pride will drive you into great temptation by the enemy. Victorious Christians achieve their success by the adherence to keeping their hearts in a state of repentance and humility before the Lord.

It is a fact that, beyond a doubt, we are living in the most exciting and extraordinary season in the history of mankind. Modern technological advancements leave us unending creative outlets of expressing our godly sentiments to the entire world. But we must realize that we are under the most significant period of transition ever, that being the transition between the final Kingdom of God's rule and reign and the cessation of worldly kingdoms as we know them. We must graciously bridge a gap that has not been successfully bridged since the world began. However, it has been prophesied in the book of Revelation that this transition will assuredly be made.

> **Then the seventh angel sounded: And there were loud voices in heaven, saying, "The kingdoms of this world have become the kingdoms of our Lord and of His Christ, and He shall reign forever and ever!"**
>
> **Revelation 11:15**

We have an opportunity to be the generation that sets this in motion, more so than any other generation preceding us.

The commonplace, subtle induction of the supernatural into our daily lifestyle, belies more than ever a failed plot of the devil. Satan meant it for his purposes, but God will tactically use it to His and our advantage in the end. Once again, He will use the enemy to advance His righteous purpose! What a tremendous opportunity is given to us. But what an awesome responsibility.

If we take full advantage of all of the technical equipment placed at our disposal, and with contrite hearts and upright minds, use it, we will display an acute sensitivity to everything that God has placed at our disposal. Then, as we press back the forces of darkness using what they think to be their own equipment (it is all really God's), we will finally announce to the world the true age in which we live.

God's timing in the installation of the final two church officers will send a death blow to the forces of darkness who have felt victorious, despite our strivings. But God will display His finest victory as we, the Church, its officers and assignees, declare that this is a prophetic, and not psychic, age.

Prophecies of the Future

The following prophesies have been given within the last ten years by the author and other prophets. It is my intention to show examples of both future and past prophecies that have or, we believe, yet will come to pass. It is my hope that they will bless you.

1983 to Present - This prophecy has come repeatedly. In another vision some years ago, God exposed sin in the Church as if He were pulling back a blanket from a bed of adulterers. (Of course, we have seen the fulfillment of aspects of this vision on our front pages and in television newscasts.) God will expose adultery and fornication, lying, mishandling of funds, and all other vices among His people. Once again, it shall be proven that the days of Ananias and Sapphira are upon us, for many have died, and will die, not recognizing the Lord's body.

1985 - A vision depicted a scene in the headquarters of the Internal Revenue Service in Washington, DC. A very officious woman brought many stacks of files and set them on the desk of a man, who swore.

He said that he was going to get "those s.o.b.'s," meaning ministers and televangelists, because they were handling too much money. The files she handed him contained names of Christian businesses and ministries. That official then set out systematically and arbitrarily to audit every tenth name.

Suddenly, the scene changed, and I saw ministers being hauled off to prison and churches padlocked, all because the church did not have its business in order. The warning from God was for churches and ministries to get their affairs in order, so that audits would not harm them.

1985 - "Germany, a wicked, cold nation, shall feel the hand of My rebuke shake her for her austere outlook. But, for the elect's sake in her, I will judge her and bring dramatic change in her, causing small coals planted within her to burst into the flames of My revival. Ministers shall be able to go back and forth between the East and the West without fear in the days to come."

Two years prior to the destruction of the Berlin wall, a well-known prophet published that the wall would come down.

1988 - Wars will rise in nations that have not been at war for many, many years. We will see blood shed around the world. We are going to see the rise of racism in the United States as we have never seen it before. These insidious forces will pale in comparison to the 60s.

There are going to be the most diabolical plots laid to bring division, strife and seditions in government and in the Church. But God will reveal each evil plot, causing victory to reign.

1989 - God is focusing on dark-skinned people, or people of color, during this time. He wants their contributions added to the Body of Christ. The Church will see the day when there will be no all black or all white congregations, by choice, but just congregations of the Lord's people. He is weaving all races, nations and classes into one common tapestry.

The United States, as well as some other countries, are taking a terrible "whipping" because of extraordinary sin. We have had more earthquakes, floods and violent storms in the last five years than there has been collectively in the last century. The earth itself is moaning and groaning, shifting and changing itself in revolt against the stench of sin and the horror of innocent blood being shed. (Rom. 8:22-25.)

1989 - It was prophesied that an eagle would rise out of the state of Arkansas. [This complete prophecy was given to President Clinton.]

1990 - The word of the Lord came, saying that youth gangs are going to turn to the Lord Jesus Christ and set up community centers, locations where young people will begin to learn about Jesus. God also is going to move in the area of mental illness. Many people do not realize how prevalent mental illness is today.

1992 - Strange occurrences of animals attacking humans will rise and make news all over the world. There will also be an attack upon our icons that we worship in the nation, namely sports figures and rock stars. There will be reported moral failures and premature death as a result of the vices of sin.

1994 - Early in the year, it was prophesied that 1994 would be a year of great reproof and shaking in the government, even involving the President. God said that He was once again going to "pull the covers back" and expose sinful and wicked things.

He said, "All those who thought they were hiding from Me, stealing, raping and pillaging My people, shall be exposed. I shall cause those sitting in high places who mock My name and think I have no power, and even speak that Christianity is dead, to stumble over their own words and fall.

"This is also the year of great and mighty men surrendering their lives to Me, for you shall hear of them falling on their faces and declaring in a loud voice without fear, that Jesus is Lord.

"This is going to be a year of restoration of the family across the nation. I am going to begin to bring home the rebellious children. I am going to begin to reunite husbands and wives, especially where one has fled from the family. I shall cause such a healing balm to flow through My people and through this nation that My voice will be heard in the nation. I will make Myself known.

"I will not be mocked in this government, but I shall cause to topple the ideas of men, and I shall lift up My standard, and begin to prepare for My return."

1994 - Pastoral caucuses and alliances will begin to help women build churches, or ministries, which has not happened with any consistency before. The prophet saw in the Spirit several Christian institutions rising, such as schools on the elementary and secondary levels, not just Bible colleges or universities

1994 - Keep your eyes focused upon the Middle East, for they have cried, "Peace, peace," but there will be no lasting peace until they say, **Blessed is He who comes in the name of the Lord** (Luke 13:35).

Constant fighting and festerings shall continue to seethe in the Middle East. Yet revival and salvation shall break forth in her as never before.

Prophecies for 1995

The following prophecies are for the year 1995 and are prepared by the author and Prophetess Paula Price, respectively. These documents were prepared without collaboration, affirming the word of the Lord, making it sure. (2 Cor. 13:1.)

The year 1995 will be a year of turbulence in governments around the world. The Middle East from Israel to Jordan to Egypt shall have an undercurrent of unrest like that of a seething pot. Christians must be as wise as serpents but as harmless as doves in this part of the world. God's Spirit is moving in an undercover fashion to bring about massive salvation.

Hatred of the U.S. will increase worldwide. The U.S. government will once again experience political upheavals. Slander and exposure of vice will become so commonplace that people will numb to it. There will be grave dissatisfaction with the status of government, particularly among minorities. God Himself will so dramatically shake the economy, that things the U.S. has relied upon for years will begin to crumble.

Frightening changes shall take place in large corporations, especially in leadership. There will be murders and thievery among the wealthy, and some will literally die from ailments directly related to the intense fear of losing wealth and power.

Also in America, we will see the infiltration of well-organized gangs stealthily creeping into the political structure. Chicago, New York, Los Angeles and several other large cities will follow suit. Simultaneously, God will move upon this same element of society with a spiritual revolution, resulting in mighty conversions and a "Holy War." Talk shows will begin to reflect the image of the false, new "clean" images of the reorganized gangs. It will be as diabolical as the syndicate operations running city governments of past decades. Gang leaders will be educated (some), street smart and politically astute, buying favors from the highest of governmental officials. The Church will be forced to act.

The movie and television industry will introduce even more blatant satanic activities, but with a new religious twist. The worship of angels will dramatically increase.

Showdowns will take place between the forces of evil and the prophets (and people) of God due to an increased awareness of spiritual activity. Beware of satanist activities and witches infiltrating the churches. But in those churches flowing under the light of God, they will not prevail as long as Jesus Christ remains Lord.

Strange weather patterns will increase worldwide through the next decade. It will be to the extent that spans of days will reflect a season that actually is not the current season. Natural and man-made disasters will weaken the economy of nations.

Beware of the I.R.S. Keep your business in order. Abstain from even the appearance of evil, washing yourselves consistently in the laver of God's Word. Then, only, will the Lord turn the delayed manifestations of blessings and begin to release the wealth of the wicked to establish His works. Don't fear; trust in God. For in all of this shaking, God will move upon His Church more gloriously than ever before, destroying her vices and exposing her prejudicial philosophies. Reconciliation shall finally begin to surface as we are pressed together through the common bonds of persecution, and there shall rise an element of the Body that will lead with great integrity.

By mid 1995, there will be a tremendous breakthrough of the Spirit of God upon the Church. The last three years of striving and pressure will all manifest in glorious victory as those things promised begin to come to pass. We will break through physically, financially and spiritually, causing tuned-in members of the Body to see their purpose as never before. God will rightly align His Church. It will be well worth waiting for.

Pam Vinnett, Author

* * *

The year 1995 will see great upheavals. Much of the loosening occurring over the last several years will break free. Many old strongholds and ancient landmarks will be torn down to make way for the new. "New wave" is the undercurrent voice as the changing of the guard, threatened for years, takes place in full swing.

The news media will be full of shock waves. Irresponsible journalism will cause it to come under attack. Discontent and a lack of public trust will force them to give up certain libertarian stances.

In business, there will be no appreciable loss, but personnel shrinkage continues as consolidation gathers momentum until the majority enterprises fall into the hand of but a few empires. Government regulations will affect this trend. Also, small businesses will suffer the fate of many small churches. Only a few will survive the next two worldwide economic crises.

Television programs that involve viewer participation in their plots and schemes loom on the horizon. Interactive systems make this possible. A strong exhibitionist spirit will take hold and facilitate this move.

In the economic arena, shock waves of every calamitous sort will rattle the comfort cages. The stage is being set for an uncanny regime that steals the hearts and pocketbooks of many nations. It emerges on the front as a sweetheart, but turns midstream (in about three years after its appearance), ushering in a vicious cycle of hatred, abuse and antisemitism, crippling several significant nations. Millions of companies will suffer and jobs by the droves will be lost.

On the home front, marriages will increase, along with reconciliations. Children will see better parenting as a result. However, as the years progress, domestic violence, seemingly driven underground by the former move, will resurface with a fervor in the latter part of the century. Emotionally unstable parents will again take their frustrations out on their offspring and a gruesome slaughter of youngsters again will prevail, starting in 1995.

An unusual criminal element, currently preparing itself to recover the souls of the nation, will surface in the latter half of the 21st century. They are well-organized and will become stronger for the underground period they were forced into by mid '95 legislation.

A shuffling of power is at present taking place in the spirit realm as principalities, in anticipation of God's next move, gear up to reassign themselves and resettle territories along unusual lines. America will suddenly find herself having to court allies for her own preservation.

The occult will become a formidable force for the Church to reckon with. Fallout from disappointment with established religion will swell its ranks. Their maneuvers will be behind the mien of the church ecumenical movement. They will deviously exert financial and social pressure on the Church in the name of keeping its brotherly love dogma, and utterly rival it in supernatural feats. A world-acclaimed and supported order of prophets will rise almost overnight. Although their rhetoric and doctrines feature the use of God's name, false salvation and conversion will permeate the theme of their message. What the Church foolishly spurns, the world will pick up and run with.

Scandals and exposures will continue in the Church. Three such will bring down some major ministries. However, many spiritual breakthroughs are on the horizon, and turnarounds of multitudinous proportions may be expected. The joy will be bittersweet. The result, supernatural healings will once again become commonplace. God will shortly manifest Himself to His Church blatantly. His Word in truth will go forth in a flurry of activity as He begins to make new demands upon established ministers and ministries. Those who have been groomed in the wilderness of alienation and rejection will be awakened with startling visions and dreams.

Elijah's fire, Paul's power, Peter's brashness and Moses' authority will resume in 1995. Clashes with the false will be so spectacular that they will make news. Conversions, spontaneous deliverances and Church enrollments will flood the Body from January onward. This period will seem much like a return to the infancy days of the Church. Also, God's favor will be upon many persecuted Davids of the faith in 1995.

Power and authority will change hands, and the astute leader will discern the times and seasons, recognizing those sent to him or her, or those set in their midst. Those refusing will see the downside of the next move of God and likely become a victim rather than a victor of it.

Be ye also ready, and those who have an ear to hear, hear what the Spirit is saying to the churches.

P. A. Price

Prophecies are sent by God to admonish or rebuke, build and restore, edify, comfort and exhort, foretell and forthtell the present and the future. They predict the desired outcome of God for individuals, churches and nations. They cry out to us of the significance of finding and abiding in the center of God's will. We should fear God, and never man, keeping in mind that all things are hinged upon His will. Otherwise, our hearts may fail us for what may be coming upon the earth.

It is not our desire to induce fear of the future, nor foster the attitude that Christians should live by prophecy. Our greatest desire is to show that God can, does and will continue to speak through the mouth of His prophets.